Gift of
Mrs. William Ewers

© DEMCO, INC.—Archive Safe

MODERN PAINTERS AND SCULPTORS
AS ILLUSTRATORS

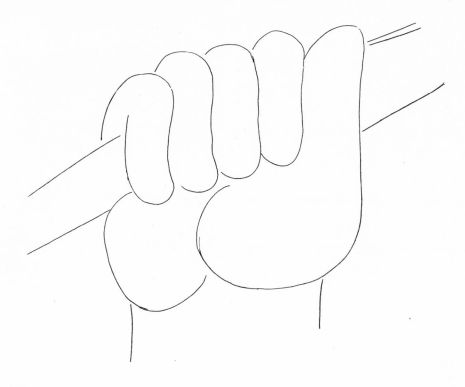

MODERN PAINTERS AND SCULPTORS

AS ILLUSTRATORS

EDITED BY MONROE WHEELER

THE MUSEUM OF MODERN ART · NEW YORK

IN ACKNOWLEDGMENT OF THE PREËMINENCE
OF THE PUBLISHER, AMBROISE VOLLARD, AND
HIS MOST GENEROUS LOAN OF RARE BOOKS
AND WORK IN PROGRESS, THE DIRECTOR OF
THE EXHIBITION TAKES PLEASURE IN DEDI-
CATING TO HIM THE PRESENT VOLUME.

TABLE OF CONTENTS

COVER: Etching by Picasso from *Les Métamorphoses d'Ovide,* Pub. by Skira.

TITLE PAGE: Etching by Matisse from *Poémes* by Mallarmé, Pub. by Skira.

ACKNOWLEDGMENTS

The Director of the Exhibition wishes to thank Miss Edith Wetmore, Mr. Philip Hofer, Mr. Ambroise Vollard, Mr. A. Hyatt Mayor, and Mr. J. B. Neumann for encouragement and counsel.

BOOKS OR ORIGINAL DRAWINGS HAVE BEEN SELECTED FROM THE FOLLOWING COLLECTIONS:

Mme. Jeanne Bucher, Paris

Mr. Jean Charlot, New York

Mr. Erich Cohn, New York

Mr. Frank Crowninshield, New York

Mr. André Derain, Paris

Marie Harriman Gallery, New York

Mr. Philip Hofer, New York

Mr. Pierre Loeb, Paris

Mme. Nadejena-Krinkin, New York

Mr. J. B. Neumann, New York

Mr. Frank Osborn, Manchester, Vt.

Mrs. Alma Reed, New York

Mr. André Dunoyer de Segonzac, Paris

Mr. John Sloan, New York

Mrs. Lloyd Bruce Wescott, New York

Miss Edith Wetmore, New York

Mr. E. Weyhe, New York

Mr. Carl Zigrosser, New York

THE FOLLOWING PUBLISHERS HAVE ALSO LENT VALUABLE MATERIAL:

The Black Sun Press, *New York;* Brentano's, Inc., *New York;* Cassell & Co., Ltd., *London;* Delphic Studios, *New York;* Philippe Gonin, *Paris;* Count G. Govone, *Paris;* Harcourt, Brace & Co., *New York;* Harper & Brothers, *New York;* Harrison of *Paris* and *New York;* M. Jacquard, Au Nouvel Essor, *Paris;* The Limited Editions Club, *New York;* The Macmillan Co., *New York;* Robert M. McBride & Co., *New York;* The Nonesuch Press, *London;* La Nouvelle Revue Française, *Paris;* Les Editions des Quatre Chemins, *Paris;* Random House, *New York;* Charles Scribner's Sons, *New York;* Galerie Simon, *Paris;* Albert Skira, *Paris;* The Society of American Bibliophiles, *New York;* The Spiral Press, *New York;* Ambroise Vollard, *Paris.*

MODERN PAINTERS AND SCULPTORS
AS ILLUSTRATORS

PICASSO, DRAWN BY COCTEAU

The word modern has at least two current meanings, and in fixing the scope of this exhibition they should be distinguished and borne in mind. The first is lexicographical, and very simple: "of the present and recent times." In general I have restricted myself to books published in the first third of the present century. Certain exceptions—work of nineteenth century painters in advance of their time—will show how our artists learned certain of their methods and inherited a portion of their inspiration from these elders, as is natural. In 1828 Delacroix published *Faust,* ideal prototype of the costly book. Regularly throughout the middle of the century appeared the popular editions illustrated by Daumier. In 1875, Manet's *Le Corbeau* (Poe's *Raven* in Mallarmé's French version) somewhat initiated his generation into a new cult of the art of the book. De Maupassant's *La Maison Tellier,* published by Vollard, at Renoir's suggestion, with compositions in various media by Degas, has only recently been given to the public, and does not seem in the least old-fashioned. For the greatest artists, as if in unconscious agreement, advance with the surest step, going very slowly, but starting decades ahead of the common flock. It is only the second-rate men who must come up-to-date in a hurry, with a thunder of theory, all upset and dishevelled as if it were the end of the world.

The word modern's second meaning is less simple. It involves many moot points of aesthetic doctrine, and is periodically obscured by the wordy and sometimes crafty pretensions of the artists themselves. It has caused a constant battle of the art-critics, and peace is not yet in sight. I mean Modern with a capital M; Modern, as one says Renaissance or Elizabethan or Baroque. One must distinguish between the crowd of commercial and academic practitioners of art in our time, and certain men who have not been content to imitate previous masters, and whose art impulse, furthermore, is reasonably free from the tendency to imitate even their own early work. At this point in the history of art, Modern may

Page 9

be taken as referring not to any one innovation, but to a large and disparate number of contemporaneous innovations; and, in each individual artist's case, to a series of them. What these men have in common is a life-long willingness to innovate, a relative freedom from aesthetic habits, good as well as bad, and some instinctive fear of ruts, and disdain for what is easy.

How many men there are who started in the vanguard fifteen or twenty years ago, whose work then was as audacious as any of their rivals', but who soon reduced their way of looking at things and rendering them to a trick and a pattern, and have plodded along ever since in the harness of their first reputation! Suppose that Picasso's career had been one long Blue Period: he would have appeared in this exhibition only if he had happened to influence younger men. And if he had not progressed beyond cubism, he would, by now, have begun to seem less truly modern than he does.

DERAIN, SELF PORTRAIT

I have restricted my present choice to the work of painters and sculptors of note *as such*—that is, I have left out of consideration books done by specialists, professional illustrators,—partly for the restriction's sake. Of course the distinction between professional and non-professional, between master of high art and publisher's employee, is an arbitrary one. No doubt the humblest engraver still somewhat pursues his early hopes of independent achievement as painter or sculptor. So I have had to resign myself to an extreme likelihood of injustice to men known to me only as illustrators. yet proud of themselves as artists. But in what other than an arbitrary spirit could I have hoped to judge the thousands of contemporary picture-books?

The by-products of a career of high art are not necessarily superior to the result of humbler specialization in work for publishers. They generally are, at least at present. A hundred years ago, Deveria and Doré, for example, did neglect their remarkable talent for oil-painting in order to do nothing but sketch and engrave and draw on stone all their lives, in the pay of publishers. There is little or no point in doing so today. Such publishers as Vollard and Skira do pay large fees for the pictorial enrichment of their volumes; but the painters whom they favor receive even more princely prices for paintings. For the sale of pictures has become more profitable than ever before. Creators of odd and even abstract beauty have made more money than the rapid, obedient hack. Even portrait-painting and the erection of public monuments have proved less remunerative than the right sort of lawlessness. For men with any of the kinds of genius that have been in fashion, book-illustration has not been tempting at all, from the economic standpoint. Yet almost all our modern celebrities have engaged in it.

Celebrated artists, ordinarily a law unto themselves, working to order, upon subject-matter dictated to them by living or dead authors, obliged also to take into account bibliophilic taste—might one not expect such an exhibition as this to reveal, above all, bad effects of pot-boiling? The exact opposite seems to be the case. There is no trace of boredom, no carelessness. I have also given some attention to the circumstances in which these various series of illustration were commissioned and executed. Aesthetically successful or not, most of the work that I have left out, and all that I have included, appears to have been undertaken by the artists with real enthusiasm, in willing collaboration with literary men who were friends of theirs, and with publishers who seemed to them friendly. There is no evidence of anyone's having thought of himself as shamefully hired, or as working at a disadvantage in harness, or as compromised either by literary or commercial taste. I honestly believe that the elimination of those whose specialty and chief source of income have been book-illustration—while conveniently reducing the number of books I had to choose from—has also automatically raised the level of excellence and the percentage of sincerity.

There is further advantage in having given all our space to all-round artists. This exhibition may be studied as a miniature survey of modern art in general. It will be possible for disinterested art-lovers to correct certain casual and critical errors about it. No one now makes the old mistake of supposing that our painters are indifferent to classic examples of their art, or generally ignorant of past methods. But many people still believe that modern art is or should be non-literary; that the best modern painters feel, not mere timidity, but repugnance, in regard to the pictorial treatment of dramatic or poetical subjects. This opinion was first regularly put forth to defend cubism when it was shocking to the public, and to be of assistance to the new generation of art-dealers in marketing it. Contrary to early expectations, cubism has failed to predominate over other schools in our epoch. But the purists' doctrine of restricted pictorial subject-matter is still constantly applied to the art of painting in general. In this exhibition we have evidence that the great men of modernism themselves, even cubists, have not consistently held this opinion, nor felt any real repugnance to the forbidden themes. On the contrary, with obvious enjoyment, they have welcomed opportunities to try their skill at legend and symbol and sentiment, adapting their style to new uses, if necessary, and accepting whatever restrictions complex subject-matter may impose.

CHAGALL, SELF PORTRAIT

A certain fanatic school of bibliophiles maintains a particular ideal of the fine book. If there are to be pictures—which many purists among them will not admit —their significance in relation to the text is judged to be of less importance than their harmony with the typeface. Here is a restriction of an uninspiring order which the important artists may be expected to resent. On this account there exists a prejudice among these fastidious collectors against real painters as illustrators. The docile professional understands them. But in reality the book which attains a perfect union of the elements involved is excessively rare. Painters and sculptors working with very patient and affluent publishers sometimes achieve it. The *Eclogae et Georgica* of Virgil that Maillol decorated for Count Kessler satisfies this prejudiced group as well as art-lovers. Rockwell Kent's original *Candide* pleases them and the general public.

In sensuous effect as combined with fine typography, and in variety of possible combinations, no mechanical process of reproduction can compare with the artist's handicraft; and the skill of experts who engrave after the artist's drawing is rarely to be trusted. This evidently occurred to a number of book-loving painters at the turn of the century, and stimulated their earliest efforts in a new direction. Throughout the eighteenth and the nineteenth centuries, the artists employed in illustration merely furnished sketches, more or less freely transcribed by engravers of extreme virtuosity. Rich collectors, rather appreciative of richness and finish than sensitive to art, gave as much credit to engraver as to artist. The magnificent illustrations in question almost entirely lack the spontaneity and forcefulness of original drawing, and seem inferior aesthetically to less accomplished graphic art of previous centuries. It happened that spontaneity and force were ruling passions of the founders of contemporary art. They disliked the Rococco and the Romantic books; among Mediaeval and Renaissance illustrators they discovered their masters.

I have included in this exhibit two or three volumes in facsimile: not, strictly speaking, illustrated books. One is a sheaf of Manet's letters, illustrated by him with vivid little water colors. One is Gauguin's *Noa-Noa* as he himself put it together: autobiographical text and pictorial odds and ends of the same daily inspiration. Another is a reproduction of an ordinary edition of the Goncourt *La Fille Elisa* which Toulouse-Lautrec decorated with original sketches. Somewhat in this spirit of improvisation the painters of this epoch set about regular illustration when asked. Strangely enough, it stimulated them to mastery of first-hand techniques. For only if they themselves drew on stone or plate, or cut in the wood, could they be sure that the qualities they prized most highly in their work would not be lost.

VOLLARD, ETCHING BY DUFY

Artists aroused by this new ideal found an eager ally in Ambroise Vollard, the greatest contemporary publisher of illustrated books. His fame is international. Eight of the finest books in the present showing are his publications. A gigantic young French colonial from the island of La Réunion, he came to Paris in 1890 to seek his fortune. Starting with Degas he became enamoured of the art of his day, and opened a picture gallery. He was one of the first dealers to sense the true greatness and the incomparable market-value of Renoir, Cézanne, van Gogh, Toulouse-Lautrec, and in due time of Picasso, Derain, Rouault, and other moderns. He made friends with his painters, stored up in his big bullet-like head every anecdote and axiom that fell from their lips, and pieced it all together in several invaluable Boswellian volumes. Meanwhile he made a fortune, buying low and selling high; he has spent it all making an early dream come true—a dream of becoming the greatest publisher of illustrated books that ever lived.

He began, in the nineties, as a publisher of prints. In 1900 he issued his first great book, Verlaine's *Parallèlement* illustrated by Bonnard, followed two years later by another Bonnard masterpiece, *Daphnis and Chloë,* with nearly a hundred original lithographs in each; volumes so fine that they have not been surpassed by Vollard's own later productions, or by anyone's. Since then, he has brought out twenty-odd volumes, varied in style, thoughtfully conceived, and painstakingly and richly executed, though not all perfectly pleasing. His stubborn insistence upon flawless impression of type, wood engraving, etching, lithograph and aquatint, made it a series ranking with the best editions of the past, and almost equal to his own exorbitant ideal. It was Vollard who fostered the extraordinary collaboration between Rouault, the great mystic painter, and Aubert, the supreme wood carver, from which resulted the *Réincarnations du Père Ubu*. When Vollard found that a man's arm was not strong enough to obtain with a hand press the extreme pressure they required, he had his printer Jourde construct a special press by means of which man's strength could be supplemented, at the moment of printing, by the strength of electricity. There are innumerable similar instances of Vollard's obstinacy and extravagance, and his desire to help his painters do their best for him.

No two—certainly no three—enthusiasts will agree upon which are Vollard's best publications. They are all fine enough for it to be a question of which artist one most admires, which books one has wished to see illustrated, and how.

ROUAULT, SELF PORTRAIT

Today we think of pictures and literature as almost opposite arts, and many who are not strict bibliophiles feel that it is unnecessary and disorderly for them to mix and overlap.

In the dim beginning of history, drawing and writing developed together as human faculties, nearly identical. Primitive man's sense of magic in nature and in his own nature probably started him representing things, and he found it useful. Certain images became alphabet.

For a long time after languages had become elaborate, pictures were still used as a sort of alternate vocabulary, for both religious and practical purposes. In a sense all art was illustration, and in that sense illustration may be said to have preceded text. First came beauty of art, and after it a conscious sense of beauty; theory came last. Thus for centuries none of our present standards occurred to anyone.

Mediaeval art, sculpture as well as painting, was mostly representation of sacred scenes to help people who could not read. In the earliest printed books, the text was usually ancient; and the first masters of woodcut provided a parallel rendering of the story—as if the ancient heroes were their contemporaries, in familiar scenes—to make it vivid, and to bring it close to the reader's experience. Later, when didactic and scientific books were printed, we find illustration used chiefly as explanation of things difficult to describe in words, as in medical treatises, herbals, manuals of venery and strategy, etc. Because it is hard to tell a man how to ride horseback, engravings were added to show him the proper posture. Travellers not only wrote accounts of savages and newly discovered lands but made engravings of what they found, or had experts make them.

Then too, the foundations of religion were being shaken, and those of modern government were being laid, by a very few important books, which were cherished accordingly by the idealistic men who could afford them. Therefore the impulse which had wrought precious reliquaries turned to the worthy embodiment of the new texts: homage paid, not to a fragment of sainted bone, but to living idea, the very substance of the future. Volumes of reasoning and scholarship, not really illustratable, were lovingly embellished, just as they were magnificently bound: to show delight in them and to make them as impressive in format as they were important in content.

Today, although there is more book-illustration than ever, almost all this traditional motive for it has gone by. In the nineteenth century, artists still labored away at herbals and bestiaries. In watercolor and woodcut Gauguin portrayed his islanders somewhat as documentation of his journal, *Noa-Noa*. He, and, let us say, Iacovleff, draughtsman-in-chief to the Citroën expeditions, are the last of a long lineage. But science grows increasingly analytical, less and less descriptive. Geography and botany and zoölogy have become secondary studies, now that we have geology and chemistry and biology. Visual knowledge of the world is cheap. The photographic lens does the drudgery that artists were once proud to do.

Only the desire to honor the writer and his work by giving it a fine format—embellishing it for embellishment's sake—seems to be the same today. Books are no longer rare, and they are of less swift and less decisive effect upon men's minds; but, old and new, certain of them are still adored, as in the Renaissance. Now that book-making is an industry like any other, books are plentiful and cheap. When they are not, it is because of a deliberate turning *away* from the common commercial product—a manifestation of wealth or intellectual aristocracy. Sometimes it is also turning *back*, characteristic of idealists and aesthetes who are disappointed in the machine age and in democratic culture: rather arbitrary emulation of masterwork of the Middle Ages or the Renaissance. A good example of this rather anti-modern modernism is Eric Gill's *Canterbury Tales,* up-to-date enough in pictorial style, but quite reactionary in concept and old-fashioned in general effect. It shows the persistent influence of William Morris, also to be observed outside England. Derain's reasons for richly decorating Vincent Muselli's *Les Travaux et les Jeux* are of a different and more personal order. As a very famous artist enthusiastic about the work of this relatively unpopular poet, he has crowned it, as it were, with a laurel-wreath of lithographs, at the same time giving it a dignified sort of advertisement.

Though cubism was so much more elaborate and intellectual an art than any previous abstract style, a wealth of pure ornament might easily have been derived from it. It is surprising that cubist artists did not produce books in their manner as floridly initialed and bordered as any Book of Hours or masterpieces of Geoffrey Tory. The series of abstractions *en manière d'introduction* in Picasso's *Chef-d'Oeuvre Inconnu* suggest what cubist book-embellishment might have been; what lively pattern such an artist might have contributed to typography. But I have been unable to discover any important publication cubistically decorated throughout. Juan Gris' contributions to books were all representational cubism; and when Picasso with his usual virtuosity turned to books, he preferred not to keep within the restricted field of the style that he had invented, but to work chiefly in the great old tradition, portraying scenes and persons as in the text.

MATISSE, SELF PORTRAIT

The highest type of illustrated book is the joint work of author and artist who are contemporaries, working as in equal collaboration; inspired by similar feeling; approaching the same subject-matter from opposite directions; dealing with it twice within the covers of the one volume. Ideally speaking, the work of either author or artist would be complete without the other: the text well worth reading, in the cheapest, barest format; the series of designs fit to stand alone, and be judged on its own merits. As they appear on equal footing, our sense of the greater importance of one or the other will depend on which of the two arts we are most sensitive to. Neither should seem to take precedence. Of course, one does precede the other, in practice; but our impression in the ideal instance is of simultaneity, as if in free enthusiasm author and painter had each created alone, and the results had just happened to coincide: an impression of spiritual unity.

This sort of book is superior to others also by virtue of its entire newness, its double contemporaneity.A new text has at least that advantage over even the greatest classics. And as the artist is the writer's contemporary, he may work in whatever style is natural to him. No sort of pastiche or archaism is called for; nor is the risk of his idiom being inharmonious with the text likely to embarrass him.

Page 16

For there is deeper kinship between modern creators than can be discovered by any nationalization of their conflicting sorts of modernism; they speak a common language even without meaning to.

I have been lucky in my borrowing for this exhibition, and this greatest type of book is so well represented that my attempt to point out its excellences will seem superfluous. First in date, and it may be first in artistic excellence, is Delacroix's *Faust*. It exemplifies what I have referred to as *seeming* collaboration, inexplicable effect of simultaneity. For, of course, Delacroix was a much younger man than Goethe, and they never met. Yet the old poet was not only deeply touched by this tribute from the young man abroad, a gratifying demonstration that his art was still "modern;" but he spoke of it as enabling him to see with his eyes Faust and Mephistopheles and Marguerite more vividly than he had dreamed of them. Bonnard's lithographs for Verlaine's *Parallèlement,* Matisse's etchings for the poems of Mallarmé, Segonzac's etchings for C. L. Philippe's *Bubu de Montparnasse,* Derain's woodcuts and Dufy's lithographs for the two novels of Apollinaire, *L'Enchanteur Pourissant* and *Le Poète Assassiné*—what more fascinating constellation, what greater glory, is to be found in the entire extent of twentieth century art?

Matisse's illustration of Joyce's *Ulysses* should have been another of these perfect collaborations. It was a great idea to bring them together: celebrities of the same generation, of similar virtuosity. There must have arisen practical difficulties, or some misunderstanding. A nobler undertaking than most of the Limited Editions Club's publications, it is by no means satisfactory. That same organization has announced another almost equally exciting project: *Main Street* illustrated by Grant Wood. It might be the most interesting American illustrated book up to date.

There is another type of book of nearly equal interest: an old text that happens to be of vital importance to us today, with illustration by a modern artist equal to the task. Each epoch requires new translations, from ancient language into its own idiom, to bring close to us once more the timeless beliefs and fictions, to "start flowing freshly for us those distant sources of our intellectual life:" a new Homer (the recent *Odyssey* of Col. Lawrence, for example), a new Montaigne, or a new Bible. Just so, in every age, new attempts must be made to visualize, that is, revisualize, legend and epic and romance; "the deities, the heroes, the immortal couples of lovers, by which it is desirable that the mind should be familiarly peopled." For, in a sense, mankind is permanently mediaeval, and always attempting as much renaissance as possible. The same classics that have been translated into every tongue again and again—the above-mentioned, the Bible, and Aesop, and Ovid, and *Daphnis and Chloë,* and *Don Quixote*—have been portrayed by innumerable artists, always. Certain nineteenth century books seem to have made places for themselves on the timeless shelf: Goethe, Balzac, two or three such in a century.

This is a less daring enterprise than the marriage of modern text with contemporary picture, and perhaps it is more generally successful. The publisher has only one worthy man to decide upon, not two. He has texts sorted out for him by the passage of time and by universal opinion; and the expense of the edition is reduced.

Of course he must discover an able artist whose literary culture is sufficient and of the right sort. However, the belief that painters generally lack literary culture appears to be based upon error as to what constitutes it. The response of the present painters to a few texts apiece may be taken as exemplary, not only for painters, but for those of us whose literary enjoyment leads in other directions. We should be proud to feel and think about books as Bonnard demonstrates that he has felt and thought about *Daphnis and Chloë,* or Picasso about the *Métamorphoses*. In any field of art or study in which the French are eminent, one finds them forever coming back to the Greeks. They never cease discovering and rediscovering them; every century is a minor Renaissance.

Artists of other nations of course have different literary appetites. We have McKnight Kauffer's elegant *Anatomy of Melancholy* and his *Don Quixote*. In England there is also periodically *The Canterbury Tales;* Eric Gill's the latest. For some reason the new English work tends toward pastiche, and timid decorative effects; their portrayal of classic story is rather embellishment than portrayal. Mr. Gill has also given us *The Four Gospels*. Perhaps, now that religion is rapidly changing place in twentieth-century life, the Bible is becoming Jewish literature. Surely the most impressive modern treatment of biblical subject is Chagall's *Le Livre des Prophètes*. He is a man of extraordinary temperament; his *Fables* of La Fontaine remind us that the seventeenth-century verse is a retelling of Aesop, and that Aesop is a lengendary story-teller, whose stories derive from archaic, probably Semitic lore. Max Slevogt is the most famous German painter-illustrator, ardent and Germanic, influenced by Delacroix and Daumier rather than by contemporary French art; his choice of texts is also suggestive, tales from the Arabian Nights, Cellini, and Mozart operas.

Naturally Balzac's *Le Chef-d'Oeuvre Inconnu* appealed to Picasso. This famous tale is the romance of an old painter's folly and glory, working for ten years on one canvas, an epitome of womanly beauty, with nothing to show for it at last but superb abstraction, meaningless in others' eyes. In story-form it is a sort of preface to cubism. It is significant of that tragi-comic episode in art-history that the great cubist master himself, in 1933, given that most appropriate text to illustrate, should have chosen to do the major part of it, not abstractly, but in romantic and representational style. Picasso's labor of love has made this publication of Vollard's one of the most beautiful books in the world.

BONNARD, SELF PORTRAIT

There is another quite usual type of illustrated book: what we may call the album-type. The artist is not always willing to do real illustration, especially since bibliophilic taste, and his own concern lest his art be betrayed in reproduction, will dictate to him graphic techniques at which he may happen not to be skillful. Ambitious publishers, excited by the successes of their rivals, are not willing to let go to waste all the drawings that lie about celebrated artists' studios or that turn up after their deaths. So there are arranged marriages of book with picture not intended to illustrate: *mariages de convenance,* and sometimes by proxy. Often a text can be found that does suit the designs that happen to be available. In the present exhibition there are a number of examples of rather undeserved success of this sort, particularly arrangements of sculptors' drawing with poetry: Despiau, Rodin. Amorous verse and voluptuous studies of the nude do go well together. But two grave difficulties arise to make this free and easy excellence rarer than one would suppose: that of method of reproduction to which I have referred, and that of placement on the page. If the best the publisher can do with the drawings that he has bought is to insert full-page reproductions every now and then between pages of the text, every true bibliophile will grumble disgustedly. It does make a second-rate book, though the drawings may be superb. Rodin's *Le Jardin des Supplices* is a famous example of this. If the publisher can compose his text around the drawings, to show them off, and if some of the drawings can be used on the printed page, and if the right font of type can be found, suitable in pattern and in color to the artist's handiwork as produced—the result may be fine, as in the case of another book with drawings by Rodin:

the *Elégies Amoureuses* recently issued by Philippe Gonin, with the coöperation of the curator of the *Musée Rodin*. But here it is the publisher who has done a major part of the illustrator's work, with scissors and paste. And at best only relative success can be achieved in this way. Compare almost any of these made-up picture-books with Bonnard's *Parallèlement,* the illustration of which is also just a series of nudes, in which it is evident that the artist bore in mind as he worked not only the subject of each poem but the Garamond italic in which it was printed, the length of the lines and the shape of the stanzas; the paper appealed to him as if it were canvas. The superiority of the latter book is a mystery, but it is obvious.

SEGONZAC, BY LUC-ALBERT MOREAU

It is easy to find reasons for France's supremacy in this sort of publication, as in modern painting in general: aesthetic, and human, and economic reasons.

There was certainly an obscure potency in the international impressions brought home after the French Revolution by émigrés and grenadiers alike. From then on their art was profoundly affected by the amateurism of the English; by the passionate Baroque, Dutch and Spanish; by the oddities of the Orient, and primitive arts and crafts. All these odd elements were thoroughly digested and mixed, in the French way. From the start their modern school of painting was cosmopolitan, more so than any other has ever been: a truly European style at last.

Young foreigners have always loved going to Paris, even to study, because of the celebrated sweetness of living there. They have enriched French society with various alien enthusiasms; and given the stay-at-home Frenchman some of the experience of venturing abroad. Certain of them have become idols of the French, innovators in French art, making Parisian modernism still more international. The Frenchman makes a fine teacher, by virtue of his ability to talk and write theory without getting drunk on it, and because he never ceases to pride himself upon being a craftsman and a prudent sensualist—rather than upon his intellectual prowess. He has taught himself more than he could teach others; most teachers do.

The characteristic French combination of general parsimony with occasional passionate extravagance has been very favorable to the development of the minor and market-inspired arts. We think of the Frenchman as a selfish, worrying little fellow, a petty realist and a fatalist—not at all the artist type. Offhand, one might expect more from the German dreamer, or the American enthusiast. But the French have been getting results, and influencing all the rest of us. Painting and sculpture are universal languages; unless one reads French for pleasure one forgets that their productivity in modern literature has been no less preëminent. Think of having had Baudelaire, Rimbaud, Mallarmé, Verlaine, Apollinaire, C. L. Philippe, Max Jacob, Colette, Gide, Valéry, Claudel, Proust, Giraudoux, and Malraux, not to mention academicians and freaks, all in one life-time! Naturally, as these two abundances met, there accumulated a rich by-product in the form of illustrated books.

SLEVOGT, DRAWN BY ORLIK

The proud Germans, while their idealism in spite of defeat lasted, and while they could still manage in bankruptcy, prided themselves upon everything of this sort. They slaved, in the German way, and spent money like princes to have illustrated books as fine as anyone's, and often the result was very fine.

It is a pity that their modern painting and sculpture were not of an older and slower indigenous growth. We find a certain amateurishness in what was conscientiously Germanic and violent and mediaeval. In the opposite schools, there is a certain provincialism in regard to Paris. But the quality and quantity of fine books published in Germany in the few years after the war was applauded all over the world; and the names of the publishers Cassirer, Count Kessler, Wiegand, and others will always figure nobly in the history of German culture.

In Russia, since the revolution, picture-books have constituted a governmental policy, and something of the mediaeval spirit has started up again: pictorial representation as a helpmate art, to make new literary culture vivid and personal, to make instruction easy, to make the great Soviet moral palatable. It is not very sumptuous. Often it is not original; the Russians are scornful of the love of novelty, as being part of the bourgeois cult of "art for art's sake."

Nearly all Russian painters and sculptors have been enticed into this government illustrating-service, including many who were prominent before the war.

Page 21

The best of their work is characterized by a sort of childish violence, simply and decoratively expressed—Moujik temperament, and French poster-technique. The wondrous prehistoric caves of Altamira in northern Spain have also cast their spell on that distant society of the future. Lately the Soviets have issued a few elaborate books, illustrated with original etchings, with an eye, no doubt, on the purse of the international bibliophile. The whole of this Russian work, as befits collectivist art, is greater than any individual part.

Where art is concerned, we Americans are a timid and idle people. Apparently education, in its effect upon the aesthetic impulse, is not all one hoped. Those who invest money in artistic enterprises, such as the publication of books illustrated by noted painters, do so faint-heartedly, too eager to get it back quickly. Feeling a natural patriotism I wished to make the showing of American material as large as I could. But I found scarcely anything that one would patriotically choose to have compared with the best foreign work. With either quality or quantity in mind, one might suppose, if one did not know better, that this were a nation of extremely low cultural level, in a period of extreme poverty. Now, as in the nineteenth century, inspiration strikingly arises, again and again, but nothing further happens. Our publishers and bibliophiles still prefer to play safe by entrusting the embellishment of books to skillful minor craftsmen. Rockwell Kent is the only one of our painters upon whom the public has lavished its favor.

I have not, needless to say, undertaken to show the work done by American artists for magazines—there is any amount of it. The question of aesthetic seriousness would arise, as the artist has only a page or two to himself, and the other pictorial contents of the magazine must seem to him deplorable. It is not difficult to find less equivocal indications of what American artists would do if there were a more considerable demand for their work as book illustrators. Why were the late Charles Demuth's subtle watercolors for Henry James' *The Turn of the Screw* and *The Beast in the Jungle* never published in book form? Or why was he not asked to do others like them for publication? There are few original American artists; and those few are rarely asked to illustrate anything. Only a handful have troubled to master the various hand-processes of graphic art. Sloan, Glackens, Luks, and a few others, are honorable exceptions. Generally cheapness and easiness seem to be the passwords.

The real causes of all this may come to light in the future; the ultimate effects surely will. We are a luxury-loving and culture-loving people, and it seems unlikely that our shortage of national arts will go on forever. If the present exhibition only reminds a number of sophisticated people to buy the foreign books they like best in it, *they* are to be congratulated. But we, as a people, will be no better off. On the other hand, if we are properly provoked by the state of affairs, all may end well.

Let us selfishly consider the example of these admirable Europeans and turn to our own salvation. We must beware of their old traditions and their new tricks. Too mimicking a love of art is the worst road to artistic fulfillment.

To encourage enjoyment of these books, I wish to suggest that no effort be made to like what seems repugnant, or to rationalize what may indeed be irrational. Furthermore, I believe this to be a necessary step in the evolution of any people in any period, toward the enthusiasm and the critical temper favorable to creation.

Artists themselves point the way, giving us the most entertaining examples of uninhibited preference. It is evident that the artist would be enfeebled in the realization of his innate excellence if he did not to some extent clear his mind of the opposite. Probably one cannot make the most of the experience of liking without indulging in some even erroneous distaste. El Greco referred to Michelangelo as a good man who, alas, could not paint. Delacroix expressed abhorrence of the austerity of Ingres, saying after a visit, "I left him in the full chill of creation." Manet said Cézanne was a bricklayer who painted with his trowel. Cézanne was impressed by nothing in Gauguin's work except the impropriety, and nothing in van Gogh's except the evidence of madness. And they were all quite right.

It is surprising how much rightness can be developed out of one's natural sensibility and common sense. Good taste is indeed a thing to be proud of, but the only real education that one's taste may be given is the good-natured exercise of it upon various works of art. Odd new works on the one hand, universally admired masterpieces on the other, give the best training. In the heaven of art there are many mansions, and in modern art particularly, a multiplicity of schools, justifying preferences and prejudices in like number, and there are odds and ends of delight for each of us, according to his spirit.

MONROE WHEELER

INDEX OF PLATES

FOR THE SAKE OF A MINIMUM REDUCTION OF THE LARGER BOOK PAGES,
THE CORRECT MARGINS ARE NOT INDICATED IN THE FOLLOWING PLATES.

45. **DEGAS**: Color etching, after drawing. De Maupassant, La Maison Tellier

72. GAUGUIN: Watercolor. Gauguin, Noa-Noa

Page 28

C'est dans la Thébaïde, au haut d'une montagne, ſur une plate-
forme arrondie en demi-lune, & qu'enferment de groſſes pierres.

La cabane de l'Ermite occupe le fond. Elle eſt faite de boue &
de roſeaux, à toit plat, ſans porte. On diſtingue dans l'intérieur une
cruche avec un pain noir; au milieu, ſur un ſtèle de bois, un gros
livre; par terre çà & là des filaments de ſparterie, deux ou trois
nattes, une corbeille, un couteau.

66. REDON: Lithograph. Flaubert, La Tentation de Saint-Antoine

L'Araignée

201. TOULOUSE-LAUTREC: Lithograph. Renard, Histoires Naturelles

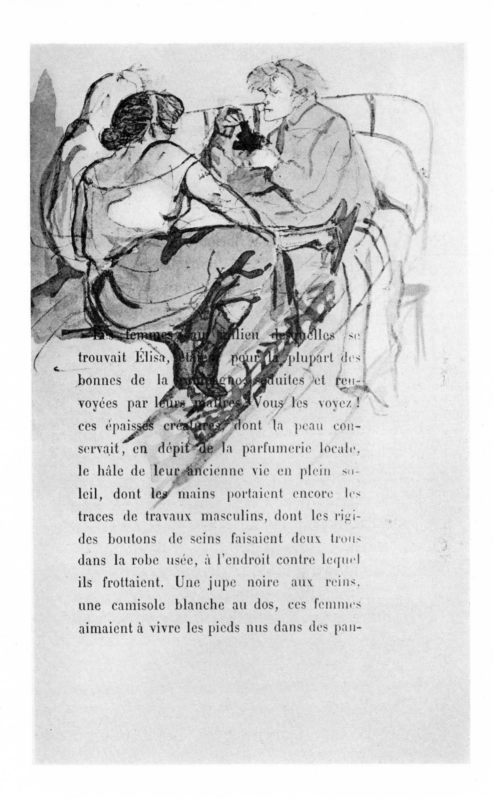

Les femmes au milieu desquelles se
trouvait Élisa, étaient pour la plupart des
bonnes de la campagne, séduites et ren-
voyées par leurs maîtres. Vous les voyez !
ces épaisses créatures, dont la peau con-
servait, en dépit de la parfumerie locale,
le hâle de leur ancienne vie en plein so-
leil, dont les mains portaient encore les
traces de travaux masculins, dont les rigi-
des boutons de seins faisaient deux trous
dans la robe usée, à l'endroit contre lequel
ils frottaient. Une jupe noire aux reins,
une camisole blanche au dos, ces femmes
aimaient à vivre les pieds nus dans des pan-

202. TOULOUSE-LAUTREC: Watercolor. E. de Goncourt, La Fille Elisa

Et dois-je le punir de m'avoir trop aimé ?
Triomphons Diomede & vantons nos foiblesses,
Nous avons sans respect attaqué deux Déesses,
Vénus fut par tes coups traitée indignement,
Et Corine aujourd'hui l'est par ceux d'un Amant.
Nos crimes sont égaux, quoi qu'avéc difference,
Le mien est pur outrage, & le tien est vaillance.
Tu servois ton païs contre des Dieux jaloux,
Et contre mon amour j'ai servi mon courroux.
Pour cet exploit si beau, cette illustre victoire
Le triomphe m'est dû si Rome m'en veut croire,
Et jusqu'au Capitole il faut porter aux Dieux
De grands remercimens d'un coup si glorieux.
On entendra les cris de mille voix Romaines
Me mettre au rang fameux de nos grands
  Capitaines ;
Et chacun sous l'apas d'un hommage moqueur
Vangera ma Maîtresse en me faisant honneur.
Corine aux yeux de Rome exposée en victime
Aux pompes de mon char attachera mon crime,
Et me reprochera dans un si triste état
Les coups d'un témeraire & les feux d'un ingrat.

 26

173. RODIN: Wood engraving. Ovid, Elégies Amoureuses

173. RODIN: Wood engraving. Ovid, Elégies Amoureuses

Eux étant ainsi occupés, vint un second mes-
sager dire qu'on vendangeât au plus tôt, et qu'il
avoit charge de demeurer là jusqu'à ce que le
vin fût fait, pour puis après s'en retourner en la
ville querir leur maître, qui ne viendroit sinon au

225

22. BONNARD: Lithograph. Longus, Daphnis and Chloë

Ne fronce plus ces sourcils-ci,
Casta, ni cette bouche-ci,
Laisse-moi puiser tous tes baumes,
Piana, sucrés, salés, poivrés,
Et laisse-moi boire, poivrés,
Salés, sucrés, tes sacrés baumes.

33

21. BONNARD: Lithograph. Verlaine, Parallèlement

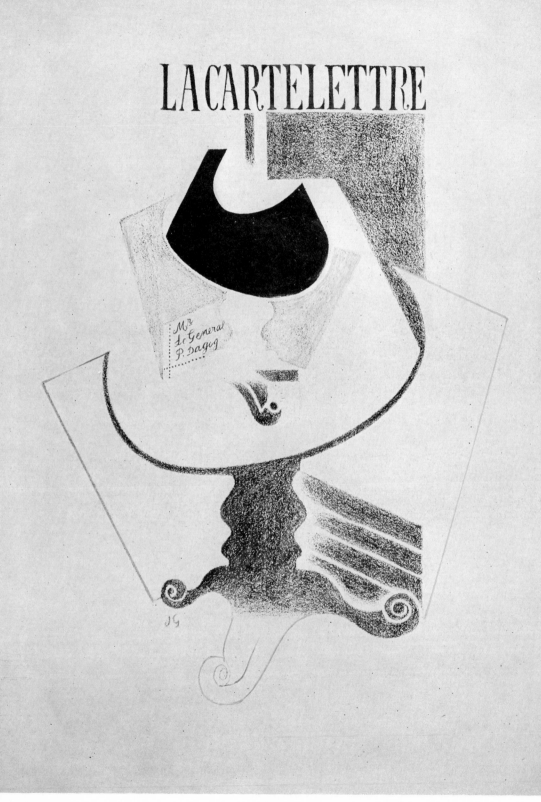

78. GRIS: Lithograph. Jacob, Ne Coupez Pas Mademoiselle

SCÈNE IX

Méduse — Astolfo — Frisette — Polycarpe

MÉDUSE

Je l'ai subjugué. (Le baron consulte le thermomètre) Comme ma vue baisse! Depuis ce matin elle a baissé de six degrés!... (Apparition d'Astolfo) Attention! Voici le moment de lui tendre mon piège. (Méduse fascine Astolfo) (A brûle-pourpoint.) Savez-vous danser sur un œil?... sur l'œil gauche?

ASTOLFO
Suffoquant de surprise.

? ...

MÉDUSE
Prenant des airs d'hypnotiseur. Durement.

Je vous demande si vous savez danser sur un œil?... sur l'œil gauche? (lui mettant l'index dans l'œil droit) sur celui-ci?

27. BRAQUE: Color wood engraving. Satie, Le Piège de Méduse

52. DERAIN: Woodcut. Apollinaire, L'Enchanteur Pourrissant

Dans un sentier de toiles, les saltimbanques
de la foire s'éveillent la nuit sous leurs draps
sales. Les hommes ont des nuques fraîches, les
cheveux des femmes, des cheveux d'occasion, sont
emmêlés sur les chemises. Le Pesage d'Auteuil
impose son diadème de bois sans chevelure.

53. DERAIN: Woodcut. Jacob, Les Oeuvres Burlesques et Mystiques du Frère Matorel

56. DERAIN: Lithograph. Muselli, Les Travaux et les Jeux

LE BOEUF.

Ce chérubin dit la louange
Du paradis, où, près des anges,
Nous revivrons, mes chers amis
Quand le bon Dieu l'aura permis.

60. DUFY: Wood engraving. Apollinaire, Le Bestiaire

62. DUFY: Lithograph. Apollinaire, Le Poète Assassiné

61. DUFY: Stencil-colored lithograph. Mallarmé, Madrigaux

ARCIN, en sa chambre d'hôtel, se rongeait. Ses réveils étaient pénibles. Ouvrant les yeux, il se retrouvait seul, dans un lit loué, au milieu d'une pièce banale, parmi des meubles qui n'étaient pas seulement laids, mais qui encore avaient l'impersonnalité triste des choses qui n'appartiennent à personne. Lui aussi était comme une épave. Il avait échoué là. Là ou ailleurs... Demain, où serait-il?... Et où il serait, pour-

63. DUFY: Etching. Montfort, La Belle Enfant

71. FRIESZ: Color wood engraving. Ronsard, Poèmes

115. LEGER: Color composition. Cendrars, La Fin du Monde

47. LHOTE: Watercolor drawing. Cocteau, Escales

175. ROUAULT: Lithograph. Arland, Carnets de Gilbert

174. ROUAULT: Lithograph. Rouault, Paysages Légendaires

177. ROUAULT: Color etching. Rouault, Le Cirque de l'Etoile Filante

RHUM

C'est pour ça qu'elle n'était pas dans la salle... Je l'ai cherchée au deuxième rang d'orchestre où le Monsieur avait dit. Elle m'attendait ici. Bravo ! C'est vrai qu'elle est gentille... *(Il l'écarte de nouveau.)* Une seconde, mon petit...

187. SEGONZAC: Etching. Gignoux, L'Appel du Clown

186. SEGONZAC: Etching. Philippe, Bubu de Montparnasse

189. SEGONZAC: Etching. Virgil, Georgiques

107. **LAURENCIN**: Color lithograph. L'Héritier de Villandon, L'Adroite Princesse

CALLIGRAMMES

ombre *Vous voilà de nouveau près de moi*
Souvenirs de mes compagnons morts à la guerre
L'olive du temps
Souvenirs qui n'en faites plus qu'un

94

35. DE CHIRICO: Lithograph. Apollinaire, Calligrammes

41. DALI: Etching. Lautréamont, Les Chants de Maldoror

IX. — LYCIDAS, MŒRIS

LYCIDAS

Où, Mœris, te portent tes pas? N'est-ce pas où mène le chemin, dans la ville?

MŒRIS

O Lycidas! n'avons-nous tant vécu que pour entendre

57

10. BEAUDIN: Etching. Virgil, Bucoliques

Je suis entré dans mon jardin, ô ma sœur, ma fiancée; j'ai récolté ma myrrhe et mon baume, j'ai mangé de mes rayons de miel, j'ai bu mon vin et mon lait... Mangez, mes

65

116. LEGRAND: Aquatint. Le Cantique des Cantiques

31. CHAGALL: Etching. Les Prophètes

○ Dans la vallée de Bamyian l'image se dresse, immense, mais en dépit de ses dimensions, incomparablement humaine. Elle fait corps avec la masse rocheuse de la falaise, elle-même creusée de mille cellules et tout imprégnée d'une vie mystérieuse. Page monumentale d'un livre occulte, sculptée dans la montagne. ○

○ Quelques fragments de peintures murales gardent une inspiration hellénistique dont il se dégage un charme délicat. Les plus beaux, aussi bien par l'aisance et la maîtrise de leur exécution que par la liberté de leur conception, sont groupés dans la voûte au-dessus de la tête du Grand Bouddha. ○

○ Curieux d'analyser plus profondément l'esprit de cet art et de conserver quelques documents sur ces peintures dont les années ne tarderont guère, malheureusement, à effacer les traces, je me résous avec émotion au métier de copiste. Sur un pliant instable perché sur le sommet convexe du crâne colossal, il faut passer de longues heures à travailler, la tête renversée, pour déchiffrer la suite

88. IACOVLEFF: Drawings. Expédition Citroën Centre-Asie

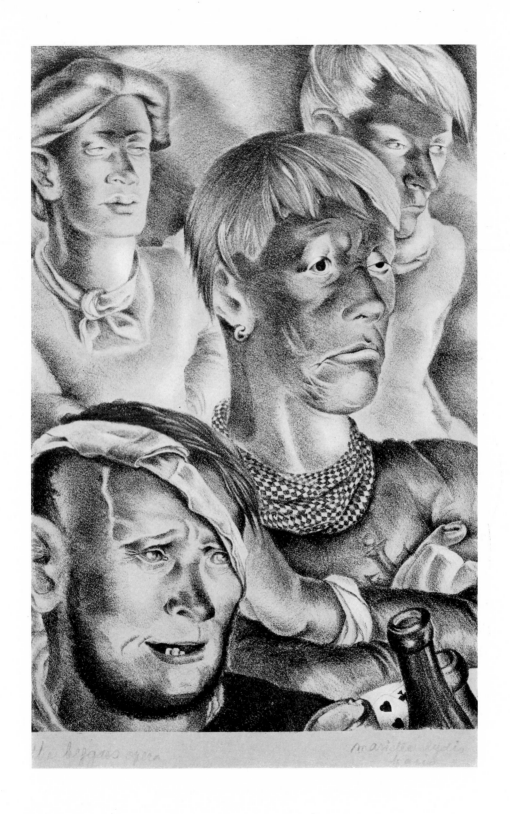

27. LYDIS: Lithograph. Gay, The Beggar's Opera

142. **MATISSE:** Etching. Mallarmé, Poèmes

LE FAVNE

C es nymphes, je les veux perpétuer.

Si clair,
Leur incarnat léger, qu'il voltige dans l'air
Assoupi de sommeils touffus.

Aimai-je un rêve?

142. MATISSE: Etching. Mallarmé, Poèmes

MANDOLINE

Les donneurs de sérénades
Et les belles écouteuses
Échangent des propos fades
Sous les ramures chanteuses.

31

105. LAPRADE: Colored engraving. Verlaine, Fêtes Galantes

JE suis belle, ô mortels, comme un rêve de pierre,
  Et mon sein, où chacun s'est meurtri tour à tour,
Est fait pour inspirer au poète un amour
Éternel et muet ainsi que la matière.

21

59. DESPIAU: Lithograph. Baudelaire, Poèmes

145. LUC-ALBERT MOREAU: Lithograph. Courières, Physiologie de la Boxe

Porbus et Pouſſin reſtèrent à la porte de l'atelier, ſe regardant l'un l'autre en silence. Si, d'abord, le peintre

de la Marie égyptienne ſe permit quelques exclamations : — Ah! elle ſe déshabille, il lui dit de ſe mettre au jour! Il la compare! Bientôt il ſe tut à l'aspeçt de

77

163. PICASSO: Wood engraving. Balzac, Le Chef-d'Oeuvre Inconnu

163. PICASSO: Etching. Balzac, Le Chef-d'Oeuvre Inconnu

164. PICASSO: Etching. Aristophanes, Lysistrata

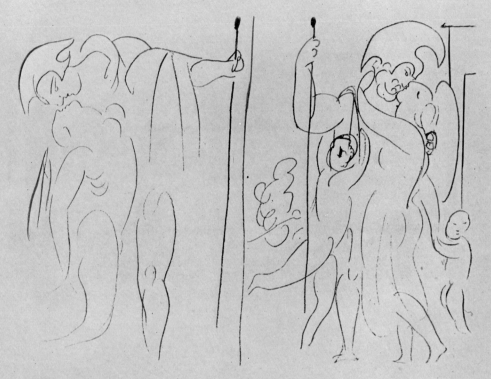

THIRD YOUNG MAN: Now won't you come down?

FIRST ATHENIAN WOMAN: Many thanks for the fillet. Perhaps I'll see you tomorrow.

FIRST YOUNG MAN: Oh, Rhodope, come down here.

THIRD ATHENIAN WOMAN: I'm afraid I can't hear you. I have grown rather deaf.

THIRD YOUNG MAN: Come down here, my darling.

FIRST ATHENIAN WOMAN: Your dancing's improved. I ought to be jealous.

Act II

Page 88

SECOND YOUNG MAN: Is there any young woman who'll take pity on a soldier?

164. PICASSO: Drawing. Aristophanes, Lysistrata

162. PICASSO: Etching. Ovid, Les Métamorphoses

141. MASSON: Etching. Desnos, C'est les Bottes de Sept Lieues

J'ai vu dans la lune
Trois petits lapins
Qui mangeaient des prunes
Comme des petits coquins.
La pipe à la bouche, le verre à la main,
En disant : « Mesdames,
Versez-nous du vin,
Tout plein ».

182. ROY: Stencil-colored wood engraving. Comptines

En cependant que la jeunesse
D'une tremoussante souplesse
Et de manimens fretillars
Agitoit les rougnons paillars
De Catin à gauche & à dextre,
Jamais ny à Clerc ny à Prestre,
Moine, Chanoine, ou Cordelier
N'a refusé son hatelier.

129. MAILLOL: Etching. Ronsard, Livret de Folastries à Janot Parisien

necdum illis labra admovi, sed condita servo.
si ad vitulam spectas, nihil est quod pocula laudes.

MENALCAS

Num quam hodie effugies; veniam quocumque vocaris.
audiat haec tantum, vel qui venit ecce Palaemon.
efficiam, posthac ne quemquam voce lacessas.

DAMOETAS

Quin age, siquid habes; in me mora non erit ulla,
nec quemquam fugio: tantum vicine Palaemon
sensibus haec imis, res est non parva, reponas.

PALAEMON

Dicite, quandoquidem in molli consedimus herba.

26

128. MAILLOL: Woodcut. Virgil, Eclogae et Georgica

191. SLEVOGT: Lithograph. Benvenuto Cellini, translated by Goethe

82. GROSZ: Drawing. Herzfelde, Tragigrotesken der Nacht

Anima

hinter der Tür, sanft

Wer sich nicht vorsieht,
Sich vermisst,
Kann den Kopf verlieren!

Hiob

verärgert

Kopf oder Welt! Eins und 's Andre!
Man zieht mir ja das Wort

14

99. KOKOSCHKA: Lithograph. Kokoschka, Hiob

Mephistopheles mit der Alten

Einst hatt' ich einen wüsten Traum;
Da sah ich einen gespaltnen Baum,
Der hatt' ein ⁓ ⁓ ⁓;
So ⁓ es war, gefiel mir's doch.

40

7. BARLACH: Woodcut. Goethe, Walpurgisnacht

Jérôme était l'homme du jour.

Le peuple norvégien lui faisait sentir de la façon la plus flatteuse l'orgueil qu'il avait à le posséder. L'Université l'invitait à prendre la parole sur Henry Becque au Grand Amphithéâtre, l'Académie Ouvrière à faire une leçon sur Barbusse, les Amis de l'Art français à traiter de la cinquième époque de Picasso. De nombreux particuliers le priaient à souper. Enfin le Directeur du Théâtre National, M. Johan Johannessen, lui adressait message sur message en

101. KROHG: Watercolor. Bedel, Jérôme

48. PAUL NASH: Colored drawing. Browne, Urne Buriall

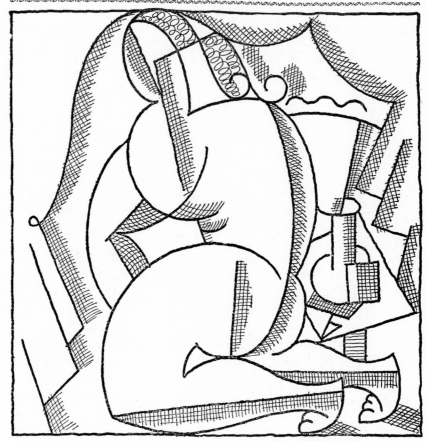

Tu cano capite amas senex nequissime
Jam plenus ætatis, animaque fœtida,
Senex hircosus tu osculare mulierem?
Utine adiens vomitum potius excuties.
Thou old goat, hoary lecher, naughty man,
With stinking breath, art thou in love?
Must thou be slavering? she spews to see
Thy filthy face, it doth so move.
Yet as some will, it is much more tolerable for an old man to marry a yong woman (our *Ladies* match they call it) for *cras erit mulier*, as he said in *Tully*. *Cato* the *Roman*, *Critobulus* in *Xenophon*, *Tyraquellus* of late, *Julius Scaliger*, &c. and many famous presidents we have in that kind; but not *e contra*: 'tis not held fit for an ancient woman to match with a yong man. For as *Varro* will, *Anus dum ludit morti delitias facit*, 'tis *Charons* match between *Cascus* and *Casca*, and the devil himself is surely well pleased with it. And therefore as the Poet inveighs, thou old *Vetustina* bed-ridden quean,

that art now skin and bones,
Cui tres capilli, quatuorque sunt dentes,
Pectus cicadæ, crusculumque formicæ,
Rugosiorem quæ geris stola frontem,
Et araenarum cassibus pares mammas.
That hast three hairs, foure teeth, a brest
Like grashopper, an emmets crest,
A skin more rugged then thy coat,
And duggs like spiders web to boot.
Must thou marry a youth again? And yet *ducentas ire nuptum post mortes amant:* howsoever it is, as *Apuleius* gives out of his *Meroe, congressus annosus, pestilens, abhorrendus*, a pestilent match, abominable, and not to be endured. In such case how can they otherwise choose but be jealous, how should they agree one with another? This inequality is not in years only, but in birth, fortunes, conditions, and all good qualities,
Si qua voles apte nubere, nube pari,
'Tis my counsel, saith *Anthony Guiverra*, to

521

90. KAUFFER: Drawing. Burton, The Anatomy of Melancholy

HERE CONTINUETH THE BOOK OF THE TALES OF CANTERBURY

'SQUIER, com neer, if it your wille be,
And sey somwhat of love; for, certes, ye
Connen theron as muche as any man.'
'Nay, sir,' quod he, 'but I wol seye as I can
With hertly wille; for I wol nat rebelle
Agayn your lust; a tale wol I telle.
Have me excused if I speke amis,
My wil is good; and lo, my tale is this.

74. GILL: Wood engraving. Chaucer, The Canterbury Tales

197. STERENBERG: Lithograph. Kipling, 40 North-50 West

Человеческая жизнь — сновидение, говорят философы-спиритуалисты, и если б они были вполне логичны, то прибавили бы: и история — тоже сновидение. Разумеется, взятые абсолютно, оба эти сравнения одинаково нелепы, однако нельзя не сознаться, что в истории действительно встречаются по местам словно провалы, перед которыми мысль человеческая останавливается не без недоумения. Поток жизни как бы прекращает свое естественное течение и образует водоворот, который кружится на одном месте, брызжет и покрывается мутной накипью, сквозь которую невозможно различить ни ясных типических черт, ни даже сколько-нибудь обособившихся явлений. Сбивчивые и неосмысленные события бессвязно следуют одно за другим, и люди, повидимому, не преследуют никаких других целей, кроме защиты нынешнего дня. Попеременно, они то трепещут, то торжествуют, и чем сильнее дает себя чувствовать унижение, тем жестче и мстительнее торжество. Источник, из которого вышла эта тревога, уже замутился; начала, во имя которых возникла борьба, стушевались; остается борьба для борьбы, искусство для искусства, изобретающее дыбу, хождение по спицам и т. д.

Конечно, тревога эта преимущественно сосредоточивается на поверхности; однакож, едва ли возможно утверждать, что и на дне в это время обстоит благополучно. Что происходит в тех слоях пучины, которые следуют непосредственно за верхним слоем и далее, до самого дна? пребывают ли они спокойными, или и на них производит свое давление тревога, обнаружившаяся в верхнем слое?—с полною достоверностью определить это невозможно, так как вообще у нас еще нет привычки приглядываться к тому, что

149

183. SAMOKHVALOV: Lithograph. Saltikov-Shedrin, Istoria Odnogo Goroda (The Story of a City)

Page 85

2. ANNENKOV: Drawing. Block, Dvenadtzat (The Twelve)

111. LEBEDEV: Lithograph. Lebedev, Verkhom (On Horseback)

137. MASEREEL: Woodcut. de Coster, Die Geschichte von Til Ulenspiegel

SLAVE SHIP

12. BENTON: Drawing. Huberman, We, the People

ROBINS M'AIME

Robins m'aime, Robins m'a,
Robins m'a demandée
Si m'ara.

Robins m'acata cotèle
D'escarlate bone et bèle,
Souskranie et chainturèle
A leur i va.
Robins m'aime, Robins m'a;
Robins m'a demandée
Si m'ara.

122. LITTLEFIELD: Original wash drawing. Porter, French Song-Book

49. DEMUTH: Original watercolor. James, The Turn of the Screw

196. SLOAN: Etching. The Works of Charles Paul de Kock

CHAPTER XXI   GOING ABOARD

IT was nearly six o'clock, but only grey imperfect misty dawn, when we drew nigh the wharf.

"There are some sailors running ahead there, if I see right," said I to Queequeg, "it can't be shadows; she's off by sunrise, I guess; come on!"

"Avast!" cried a voice, whose owner at the same time coming close behind us, laid a hand upon both our shoulders, and then insinuating himself between us, stood stooping forward a little, in the uncertain twilight, strangely peering from Queequeg to me. It was Elijah.

"Going aboard?"

⟵ 143 ⟶

96. KENT: Drawing. Melville, Moby Dick

171. ROBINSON: Drawing. Dostoyevsky, The Idiot

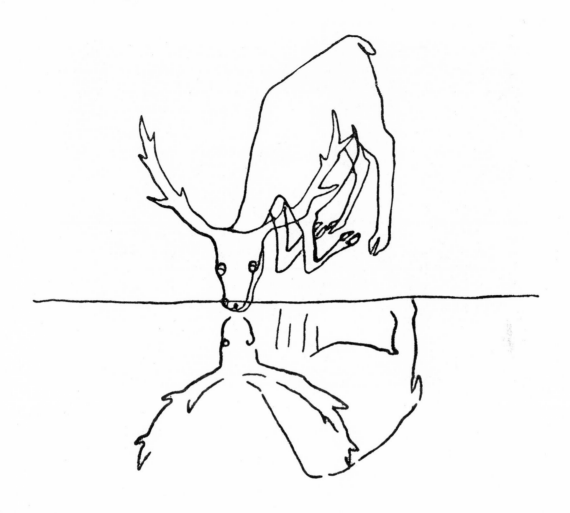

A STAG DRINKING

AS a stag was drinking upon the bank of a clear stream, he
saw his image in the water, and entered into this contem-
plation upon't. Well! says he, if these pityful shanks of mine

29. CALDER: Drawing. L'Estrange, Fables of Aesop

Page 95

212. WOOD: Crayon drawing. Horn, The Farm on the Hill

CATALOG

A star (*) before a catalog number indicates that the item is illustrated by a plate which bears the same number. Further biographical notes on many of the artists may be found in catalogs previously published by the Museum of Modern Art, New York.

NATAN ISAYEVICH ALTMAN

Painter. Born Vinnitza, Russia, 1889. Lived in Moscow in 1930.

1. Aseev: Krasnosheika (Red-neck). Giz. Leningrad. 1929. Drawings.

V. ANNENKOV

Painter. Russian contemporary.

*2. Block: Dvenadtzat (The Twelve). Alkonost. Petersburg. 1918. Drawings.

3. Chukovskii: Moí Do Dyr (Wash Till It Hurts). Giz. Leningrad. 1930. Drawings.

PEGGY BACON

Graphic artist, illustrator, writer. Born Ridgefield, Conn., 1895. Lives in New York.

4. Untermeyer and Mannes: New Songs for New Voices. Harcourt, Brace. New York. 1928. Drawings.

5. Bacon: Cat Calls. McBride. New York. 1935. Drawings.

ERNST BARLACH

Sculptor. Born Wedel near Hamburg, Germany, 1870. Lives at Güstrow, north Prussia.

6. Barlach: Der Arme Vetter. P. Cassirer. Berlin. 1919. Lithographs .

*7. Goethe: Walpurgisnacht. P. Cassirer. Berlin. 1923. Woodcuts.

8. Goethe: Gedichte. P. Cassirer. Berlin. 1924. Lithographs.

9. Schiller: An die Freude. P. Cassirer. Berlin. 1927. Woodcuts.

ANDRE BEAUDIN

Painter. Born Menecy (Seine-et-Marne), France, 1895. Studied, *Ecole des Arts Decoratifs,* until 1915. First exhibition, Paris, 1923. Lives near Paris.

*10. Virgil: Bucoliques. Skira. Paris. 1935. Etchings.

GEORGE WESLEY BELLOWS

Painter, graphic artist. Born Columbus, Ohio, 1882. Died New York, 1925.

11. Byrne: The Wind Bloweth. Century. New York. 1922. Drawings.

THOMAS HART BENTON

Painter. Born Neosho, Missouri, 1889. Lived in New York until 1935; lives at present in Kansas City, Missouri.

*12. Huberman: We, the People. Harper. New York. 1932. Drawings.

EUGENE BERMAN

Painter. Born St. Petersburg, 1899. Lives in Paris.

    13. Hugniet: Le Droit de Vareche. Au Sans Pareil. Paris. 1922. Lithographs.

EMILE BERNARD

Painter, writer. Born Lille, France, 1868. Lives in Paris.

    14. Ronsard: Les Amours de Ronsard. Vollard. Paris. 1915. Copper and wood engravings.

    15. Villon: Oeuvres Complètes. Vollard. Paris. 1918. Drawings.

    16. Les Petites Fleurs de Saint-François. Vollard. Paris. 1928. Drawings.

    17. Homer: L'Odysée. Vollard. Paris. 1930. Drawings.

GEORGII NIKOLAYEVICH BIBIKOV

Painter. Born, 1908. Studied, Red Army Art Studio, Omsk, 1919. Lived in Leningrad in 1933.

    18. Marshak: Voinas Dneprom (War with the Dnieper). Ogiz-Molodia Gvardia. Leningrad. 1931. Drawings.

IVAN YAKOVLEVICH BILIBIN

Painter. Born St. Petersburg, 1876. Studied, School of Society for the Promotion of the Fine Arts, St. Petersburg. Lives in Paris.

    19. Vol'ga (folk tale). Golike Vil'borg. Leningrad. 1904. Color drawings.

    20. Pushkin: Skazka O Tzare Saltane (The Story of Tzar Saltan). Expeditzia Zagotovlenia Gosudarstvennikh Bumag. St. Petersburg. 1905. Color drawings.

PIERRE BONNARD

Painter. Born Paris, 1867. Lives in Paris.

    *21. Verlaine: Parallèlement. Vollard. Paris. 1900. Lithographs.

    *22. Longus: Daphnis and Chloë. Vollard. Paris. 1902. Lithographs.

    23. Gide: Le Prométhée Mal Enchainé. Nouvelle Revue Française. Paris. 1920. Drawings.

    24. Mirbeau: Dingo. Vollard. Paris. 1928. Etchings.

    25. Vollard: Sainte Monique. Vollard. Paris. 1930. Lithographs, etchings and wood engravings.

EMILE-ANTOINE BOURDELLE

Sculptor, painter. Born Montauban (Tarn-et-Garonne), France, 1861. Died Vésinet (Seine-et-Oise), 1929.

    26. Mardrus: La Reine de Saba. Société Littéraire de France. Paris. 1922. Water-colors.

GEORGES BRAQUE

Painter. Born Argenteuil (Seine-et-Oise), France, 1882. Lives in Paris.

*27. Satie: Le Piège de Méduse. Galerie Simon. Paris. 1921. Color wood engravings.

28. Hesiod: Poèmes. Vollard. Paris. n.d. Etchings.

ALEXANDER CALDER

Sculptor, constructivist. Born Philadelphia, 1898. Lives in New York.

*29. L'Estrange: Fables of Aesop. Harrison of Paris. Paris. 1931. Drawings.

MARC CHAGALL

Painter. Born Vitebsk, Russia, 1887. Lives in Paris.

30. Gogol: Les Ames Mortes. Vollard. Paris. 1926. Etchings.

*31. Les Prophètes. Vollard. Paris. In preparation. Etchings.

32. La Fontaine: Les Fables. Vollard. Paris. In preparation. Etchings.

JEAN CHARLOT

Painter. Born Paris, 1898, of Franco-Russian parents. Has lived in New York since 1928.

33. Claudel: Picture Book. Becker. New York. 1933. Color lithographs.

GIORGIO DE CHIRICO

Painter. Born Volo, Greece, 1888, of Italian parents. Lives in Paris.

34. Cocteau: Le Mystère Laïc. Les Quatre Chemins. Paris. 1928. Drawings.

*35. Apollinaire: Calligrammes. Librairie Gallimard (N.R.F.). Paris. 1930. Lithographs.

36. Cocteau: Mythologie. Les Quatre Chemins. Paris. 1934. Lithographs.

LOVIS CORINTH

Painter. Born Tapiau (East Prussia), 1858. Studied, Königsberg Academy, 1876-80; Munich under Loefftz, 1880-84; *Académie Julian,* Paris, under Bouguereau and Robert Fleury, 1884-87. Königsberg, 1888-1891. Munich, 1900. Berlin and Walchensee after 1900. Died Zandvoort, Holland, 1925.

37. Das Buch Judith. Pan-Presse. Berlin. 1910. Color lithographs.

38. Luther: Autobiography. Gurlitt. Berlin. 1921. Lithographs.

39. Schiller: Wallensteins Lager. Tillgner. Berlin. 1922. Etchings.

40. Schiller: Wilhelm Tell. Nierendorf. Berlin. n.d. Color lithographs.

SALVADOR DALI

Painter. Born Figueras (Catalonia), 1904. Lives in Paris.

*41. Lautréamont: Les Chants de Maldoror. Skira. Paris. 1935. Etchings.

HONORE-VICTORIN DAUMIER

Painter, sculptor, graphic artist. Born Marseilles, 1808. Died Valmondois, 1879.

42. Philipon: Robert-Macaire. Aubert. Paris. 1839. Hand-colored wood engravings, after drawings.

43. Huart: Muséum Parisien. Beauger. Paris. 1841. Wood engravings, after drawings.

44. de Kock: La Grande Ville. Au Bureau Centrale des Publications Nouvelles. Paris. 1842. Wood engravings, after drawings.

HILAIRE-GERMAIN-EDGAR DEGAS

Painter, sculptor, graphic artist. Born Paris, 1834. Died Paris, 1917.

*45. de Maupassant: La Maison Tellier. Vollard. Paris. 1934. Etchings, after drawings.

46. Lucien (Louÿs, translator): Mimes des Courtisanes. Vollard. Paris. 1935. Etchings, after monotypes.

47. Valéry: Degas, Danse, Dessin. Vollard. Paris. In preparation. Etchings, after drawings.

FERDINAND-VICTOR-EUGENE DELACROIX

Painter. Born Charenton-Saint-Maurice (Seine), France, 1798. Died Paris, 1863.

48. Goethe: Faust I. Charles Motte. Paris. 1828. Lithographs.

48A. Two original drawings for *Faust,* lent by Philip Hofer, New York.

CHARLES DEMUTH

Painter. Born Lancaster, Pennsylvania, 1883. Died Lancaster, 1935.

*49. James: The Turn of the Screw. Unpublished. Four original watercolors, 1918, lent by Frank Osborn, Manchester, Vermont.

MAURICE DENIS

Painter. Born Granville (Manche), France, 1870. Studied, *Académie Julian,* 1888; *Ecole des Beaux-Arts.* First exhibition, 1890. Lives in Paris.

50. L'Imitation de Jésus-Christ. Vollard. Paris. 1903. Wood engravings, after drawings.

51. Verlaine: Sagesse. Vollard. Paris. 1911. Color wood engravings, after drawings.

ANDRE DERAIN

Painter. Born Chatou (Seine-et-Oise), France, 1880. Lives in Paris.

*52. Apollinaire: L'Enchanteur Pourrissant. Galerie Simon. Paris. 1909. Woodcuts.

*53. Jacob: Les Oeuvres Burlesques et Mystiques du Frère Matorel. Kahnweiler. Paris. 1912. Woodcuts.

54. Gabory: Le Nez de Cléopatre. Galerie Simon. Paris. n.d. Dry point etchings.

55. Salmon: Le Calumet. Nouvelle Revue Française. Paris. 1920. Wood engravings.

*56. Muselli: Les Travaux et les Jeux. Pouterman. Paris. 1929. Lithographs.

56A. Original drawings for *Les Travaux et les Jeux,* lent by André Derain, Paris.

57. Petronius: Satyricon. Vollard. Paris. n.d. Line engravings.

58. La Fontaine: Fables. Vollard. Paris. In preparation. Lithographs.

CHARLES DESPIAU

Sculptor. Born Mont-de-Marsan, France, 1874. Lives in Paris.

*59. Baudelaire: Poèmes. Gonin. Paris. 1935. Lithographs.

59A. *Raoul Dufy.* Apollinaire: Le Bestiaire, first edition. Deplanche. Paris. 1911. Wood engravings.

DUFY

in Paris.

*60. Apollinaire: Le Bestiaire. La Sirène. Paris. 1919. Wood engravings.

60A. Original drawings for *Le Bestiaire,* lent by Philip Hofer, New York.

*61. Mallarmé: Madrigaux. La Sirène. Paris. 1920. Stencil-colored lithographs.

*62. Apollinaire: Le Poète Assassiné. Au Sans Pareil. Paris. 1926. Lithographs.

*63. Montfort: La Belle Enfant. Vollard. Paris. 1930. Etchings.

64. Herriot: La Normandie. Vollard. Paris. In preparation. Artist's lay-out.

MAX ERNST

Painter, illustrator. Born Brühl, near Cologne, Germany, 1891. Lives in Paris.

65. Eluard: Les Malheurs des Immortels. Librairie Six. Paris. 1922. Drawings.

66. Crevel: Mr. Knife and Mrs. Fork. Black Sun Press. Paris. 1931. Photograms.

WHARTON ESHERICK

Painter. Born Philadelphia, 1887. Lives at Paoli, Pennsylvania.

67. Whitman: As I Watched the Plowman Plowing. Franklin. Philadelphia. 1927. Wood engravings.

ERNEST FIENE

Painter. Born Elberfeld, Germany, 1894. Lives in New York.

68. Breton: Phillida and Coridon. Spiral Press. New York. 1927. Color drawings.

69. Gaborse: The Story of Phaethon. Society of American Bibliophiles. New York. 1932. Watercolor drawings.

JEAN-LOUIS FORAIN

Painter. Born Rheims, 1852. Died Paris, 1931.

70. Coquiot: Les Pantins de Paris. Blaizot. Paris. 1920. Drawings in black and in color.

EMILE-OTHON FRIESZ

Painter. Born Le Havre, France, 1879. Lives in Paris.

*71. Ronsard: Poèmes. Gonin. Paris. 1934. Color wood engravings.

EUGENE-HENRI-PAUL GAUGUIN

Painter, sculptor, graphic artist. Born Paris, 1848. Died Marquesas Islands, 1903.

*72. Gauguin: Noa-Noa. Marees Gesellschaft. Berlin. 1926. Facsimile manuscript with watercolors and woodcuts.

HUGO GELLERT

Painter, illustrator. Born Budapest, 1892. Lives in New York.

73. Marx: Capital. Long & Smith. New York. 1934. Lithographs (reproductions).

ERIC GILL

Sculptor. Born Brighton, England, 1882. Art school, Chichester, under George Herbert Catt. Studied architecture, London. First sculpture, 1910. Lives at High Wycombe, England.

*74. Chaucer: The Canterbury Tales. Golden Cockerel Press. Waltham Saint Lawrence. 1929. Wood engravings.

74A. Original drawings for *The Canterbury Tales,* lent by Philip Hofer, New York.

75. The Four Gospels. Golden Cockerel Press. Waltham Saint Lawrence. 1931. Drawings.

75A. Original drawings for *The Four Gospels,* lent by Philip Hofer, New York.

WILLIAM J. GLACKENS

Painter, illustrator. Born Philadelphia, 1870. Lives in New York.

76. Norris, translator: The Works of Charles Paul de Kock. Quinby. New York. 1903-05. Etchings.

JUAN GRIS

Painter, illustrator. Born Madrid, 1887. Died Paris, 1927.

77. Stein: A Book. Galerie Simon. Paris. n.d. Lithographs.

*78. Jacob: Ne Coupez Pas Mademoiselle. Galerie Simon. Paris. 1921. Lithographs.

79. Radiguet: Denise. Galerie Simon. Paris. n.d. Lithographs.

80. Salacion: Le Casseur d'Assiettes. Galerie Simon. Paris. n.d. Lithographs.

MARCEL GROMAIRE

Painter. Born Noyelles-sur-Sambre (Nord), France, 1892. Studied, Paris, *Lycée Buffon;* and other schools. Lives in Paris.

81. Baudelaire: Petits Poèmes en Prose. Les Quatre Chemins. Paris. 1926. Etchings.

GEORGE GROSZ

Painter, illustrator. Born Berlin, 1893. Has lived in New York since 1932.

*82. Herzfelde: Tragigrotesken der Nacht. Malik-Verlag. Berlin. 1920. Drawings.

83. Dos Passos: Interregnum. Black Sun Press. New York. 1936. Drawings and lithograph.

83A. Two original drawings for *Interregnum*, lent by Mrs. Erich Cohn and the Black Sun Press, New York.

84. O. Henry: The Voice of the City. Limited Editions Club. New York. 1935. Watercolors.

JEAN HUGO

Painter. Born Paris, 1894. Lives in France.

85. Cocteau: Roméo et Juliette. Au Sans Pareil. Paris. 1926. Colored drawings.

86. Bibesco: Le Perroquet Vert. Editions Jeanne Walter. Paris. 1929. Colored lithographs.

87. Maurois: Climats. "Le Livre." Paris. 1929. Gouaches.

ALEXANDRE IACOVLEFF

Painter. Born St. Petersburg, 1887. Studied, Academy of Fine Arts, St. Petersburg, until 1913; then Italy. China, Mongolia, Japan, 1917-20. Paris, 1920. Artist to Citroën African expedition, 1924; Asiatic expedition. At present, teacher at School of the Museum of Fine Arts, Boston.

*88. Iacovleff: Expédition Citroën Centre-Asie. Meynial. Paris. n.d. Paintings and drawings.

VASILY KANDINSKY

Painter. Born Moscow, 1866. Has lived in Paris since 1934.

89. Kandinsky: Klänge. Piper. Munich. n.d. Color woodcuts.

EDWARD McKNIGHT KAUFFER

Painter, commercial artist, illustrator. Born Great Falls, Montana, 1891. Studied, Art Institute of Chicago, and in Munich. Has lived in London since 1914.

*90. Burton: The Anatomy of Melancholy. Nonesuch Press. London. 1925. Drawings.

91. Bennett: Robinson Crusoe. Etchells & Macdonald. London. 1929. Color drawings.

92. Cervantes: Don Quixote. Nonesuch Press. London. 1930. Watercolors.

ROCKWELL KENT

Painter, graphic artist, illustrator. Born Tarrytown Heights, New York, 1882. Lives at Ausable Forks, New York.

93. Kent: Wilderness. Putnam's. New York. 1920. Drawings.

94. Kent: Voyaging. Putnam's. New York. 1924. Drawings.
95. Voltaire: Candide. Random House. New York. 1928. Drawings.
*96. Melville: Moby Dick. Lakeside Press. Chicago. 1930. Drawings.

ERNST LUDWIG KIRCHNER

Painter. Born Aschoffenburg (Bavaria), 1880. Has lived since 1918 at Frauenkirche, near Davos, Switzerland.

97. Döblin: Das Stiftsfräulein und der Tod. Meyer. Berlin. 1913. Woodcuts.
98. Heym: Umbra Vitae. Wolff. Munich. 1924. Woodcuts.

OSKAR KOKOSCHKA

Painter. Born Pöchlarn, Austria, 1886.

*99. Kokoschka: Hiob. P. Cassirer. Berlin. 1917. Lithographs.
100. Kokoschka: Der Gefesselte Columbus. Gurlitt. Berlin. 1921. Lithographs; text lithographed by E. R. Weiss.

PER KROHG

Painter. Born Christiania, Norway, 1889. Lives in Paris.

*101. Bedel: Jérôme. Librairie Gallimard (N.R.F.). Paris. 1929. Watercolors.

V. KRUKOV

Painter. Russian contemporary.

102. Trevoga (Alarm). Kultura. Kiev. n.d. Drawings.
103. Kotzubinski: Dvikizochki (Two Little Goats). Kultura. Kiev. 1930. Drawings.

ROGER DE LA FRESNAYE

Painter. Born Le Mans (Sarthe), France, 1885. Lives in Paris.

104. Gide: Palludes. Nouvelle Revue Française. Paris. 1921. Lithographs.

PIERRE LAPRADE

Painter. Born Narbonne (Aude), France, 1875. Studied, Bourdelle's studio at Montauban. Holland, 1906. Italy, 1907. Settings for Ravel ballet, *Pygmalion*. Died, 1931.

*105. Verlaine: Fêtes Galantes. Vollard. Paris. 1930. Etchings and colored engravings.

MARIE LAURENCIN

Painter. Born Paris, 1885. Lives in Paris.

106. Gide: La Tentative Amoureuse. Nouvelle Revue Française. Paris. 1921. Color wood engravings by Jules Germain, after watercolors by Marie Laurencin.
*107. L'Héritier de Villandon: L'Adroite Princesse ou les Aventures de Finette. Tremois. Paris. 1928. Color lithographs.

VLADIMIR VASILEVICH LEBEDEV

Painter, illustrator, poster designer. Born St. Petersburg, 1891. Lived in Leningrad in 1934.

108. Pushkin: Contes Populaires Russes. Société Littéraire de France. Paris. 1919. Colored wood engravings.

109. Kipling (Chukovski, translator): Slonenok (How the Elephant Got His Trunk). Gosudarstvnnaya Tipografia. Leningrad. 1922. Drawings.

110. Marshak: Glupiĭ Mishenok (Foolish Little Mouse). Giz. Leningrad and Moscow. 1928. Drawings.

*111. Lebedev: Verkhom (On Horseback). Giz. Leningrad. 1929. Lithographs.

112. Marshak: Doska-Sorevnovania (The Blackboard of Competition). Molodaya-Gvardia. Leningrad. 1931. Drawings.

113. Marshak: Pudel (The Poodle). Giz. Leningrad. 1931. Drawings.

113A. Marshak: Progulka Na Osle (Joy Ride on a Mule). Moscow & Leningrad, 1932. Lithographs.

FERNAND LEGER

Painter. Born Argentan (Orne), France, 1881. Lives in Paris.

114. Malraux: Lunes en Papier. Galerie Simon. Paris. n.d. Wood engravings.

*115. Cendrars: La Fin du Monde. La Sirène. Paris. 1919. Color compositions.

EDY LEGRAND

Painter, illustrator. Born Bordeaux, France, 1893. Studied, Switzerland; Italy; Munich; *Ecole des Beaux-Arts,* Paris, 1912. French army, 1914-20. Has painted in Switzerland, Corsica, Provence, North Africa. Lives in Paris.

*116. Le Cantique des Cantiques. Editions Orion. Paris. 1930. Aquatints.

ANDRE LHOTE

Painter, writer. Born Bordeaux, France, 1885. Lives in Paris.

*117. Cocteau: Escales. La Sirène. Paris. 1920. Colored drawings.

MAX LIEBERMANN

Painter. Born Berlin, 1847. Studied, Academy at Weimar, 1868. Düsseldorf, 1870; influenced by Munkacsy. Paris, 1872-78; influenced by Courbet, Millet, Corot. Berlin, 1884. Founder with Leistikow of Berlin "Secession," 1898. President, Prussian Academy of Arts, 1920-33, when he resigned as anti-Nazi protest. Died Berlin, 1935.

118. Bie: Holländisches Skizzenbuch. Bard. Berlin. 1911. Drawings and lithograph.

119. Goethe: Gedichte. P. Cassirer. Berlin. 1924. Lithographs.

120. Kleist: Kleine Schriften. P. Cassirer. Berlin. n.d. (192-.) Lithographs.

EL LISSITZKY

Painter, constructivist, architect, editor. Born Smolensk, Russia, 1890. Lives in Moscow.

121. Pro 2 □. V. Mayakovski. n. d. Drawings.

WILLIAM HORACE LITTLEFIELD

Painter, lithographer. Born Roxbury, Massachusetts, 1902. Lives in Boston.

*122. Porter: French Song-Book. Harrison of Paris. Paris. 1933. Original wash drawings (unique copy).

JEAN LURÇAT

Painter. Born Paris, 1892. Lives in Paris.

123. Cingria: Les Limbes. Bucher. Paris. 1930. Dry point etchings.

MARIETTE LYDIS

Painter, illustrator. Born Vienna, 1894. Lives in Paris.

124. Baudelaire: Les Fleurs du Mal. Edition Govone. Paris. 1928. Colored drawings.

125. Ovid: L'Art d'Aimer. Edition Govone. Paris. 1931. Lithographs.

126. Le Livre de Marco Polo. Les Cent Une. Paris. 1932. Color etchings.

*127. Gay: The Beggar's Opera. Limited Editions Club. New York. In preparation. Lithographs.

ARISTIDE MAILLOL

Sculptor. Born Banyuls-sur-Mer (Pyrénées Orientales), France, 1861. Lives at Marly, near Paris.

*128. Virgil: Eclogae et Georgica. Insel-Verlag. Leipzig. 1926. Woodcuts.

*129. Ronsard: Livret de Folastries à Janot Parisien. Vollard. Paris. 1933. Etchings.

130. Ovid: L'Art d'Aimer. Gonin. Paris. 1935. Lithographs and woodcuts.

131. Longus: Daphnis & Chloë. Gonin. Paris. 1936. Original woodcuts.

EDOUARD MANET

Painter. Born Paris, 1832. Died Paris, 1883.

132. Poe (Mallarmé, translator): Le Corbeau. Lesclide. Paris. 1875. Lithographs (wash drawings transferred to stone).

133. Manet: Lettres (facsimile). Legarrec. Paris. n.d. Watercolors.

LOUIS MARCOUSSIS

Painter, etcher. Born Warsaw, Poland, 1883. Lives in Paris.

134. Tzara: L'Indicateur des Chemins de Coeur. Bucher. Paris. 1928. Etchings.

FRANS MASEREEL

Painter, graphic artist. Born Blankenberghe, Belgium, 1889. Lives in Paris.

135. Vermeylen: Der Ewige Jude. Insel-Verlag. Leipzig. 1921. Woodcuts.

136. Verhaeren: Le Travailleur Etrange. Editions du Sablier. Paris. 1921. Woodcuts.

*137. de Coster: Die Geschichte von Til Ulenspiegel. Wolff. Munich. 1926. Woodcuts.

138. Morand: Lampes à Arc. Kieffer. Paris. 1927. Lithographs.

ANDRE MASSON

Painter, illustrator. Born Balagny (Oise), France, 1896. Lives in Paris.

139. Limbour: Soleils Bas. Galerie Simon. Paris. 1924. Dry point etchings.

140. Leiris: Simulacre. Galerie Simon. Paris. 1925. Lithographs.

*141. Desnos: C'Est les Bottes de Sept Lieues. Galerie Simon. Paris. 1926. Etchings.

HENRI-MATISSE

Painter, sculptor. Born Le Cateau (Le Cateau), France, 1869. Lives in Nice.

*142. Mallarmé: Poèmes. Skira. Lausanne. 1932. Etchings.

143. Joyce: Ulysses. Limited Editions Club. New York. 1935. Etchings and drawings.

JOAN MIRO

Painter. Born Montroig, near Barcelona, 1893. Lives at Montroig.

144. Hirtz: Il Etait une Petite Pie. Bucher. Paris, 1928. Color drawings.

LUC-ALBERT MOREAU

Painter. Born Paris, 1882. Lives in Paris.

*145. Courières: Physiologie de la Boxe. Librairie Floury. Paris. 1929. Lithographs.

JOHN NORTHCOTE NASH

Painter. Born London, 1893. Lives at Aylesbury (Bucks), England.

146. Dallimore: Poisonous Plants. Etchells & Macdonald. London. 1927. Wood engravings.

PAUL NASH

Painter. Born London, 1889. Studied, Slade School, London. Professor, Royal College of Art, 1924-25. Lives in London.

147. Genesis: Nonesuch Press. London. 1924. Wood engravings.

*148. Browne: Urne Buriall. Cassell. London. 1932. Colored drawings.

IGNATII IGNATIEVICH NIVINSKI

Painter, designer for theatre. Born Moscow, 1880. Professor of etching, High School of Art and Industry, Moscow. Lived in Moscow in 1930.

149. Goethe: Rimskie Elegii (Roman Elegy). Academia. Moscow and Leningrad. 1933. Etchings and drawings.

JOSE CLEMENTE OROZCO

Painter. Born Zapotlan (Jalisco), Mexico, 1883. Lives at present at Guadalajara (Jalisco).

150. Azuela: Underdogs. Brentano. New York. 1929. Drawings.

150A. Two original drawings for *Underdogs,* lent by Mrs. Alma Reed, New York.

151. Susan Smith: Glories of Venus. Harper. New York. 1931. Drawings.

151A. Two original drawings for *Glories of Venus,* lent by Mrs. Alma Reed, New York.

JULES PASCIN

Painter. Born Widden, Bulgaria, 1885. Suicide Paris, 1930.

152. Heine: Aus den Memoiren des Herrn von Schnabelewopsky. P. Cassirer. Berlin. 1910. Lithographs.

153. Perrault: Cendrillon (Cinderella). Tremois. Paris. n.d. Color engravings and drawings.

154. Warnod: Trois Petites Filles dans la Rue. Fanfare de Montparnasse. Paris. 1925. Watercolors.

155. Morand: Fermé la Nuit. Nouvelle Revue Française. Paris. 1925. Colored etchings and drawings.

MAX PECHSTEIN

Painter. Born Zwickau, Germany, 1881.

156. Das Vater Unser (The Lord's Prayer). Propyläen. Berlin. 1921. Woodcuts.

PETRENKA

Painter. Russian contemporary.

157. Benneliki: Zagaslii Likhtar. Kultura. Kiev. 1930. Drawings.

PABLO PICASSO

Painter, sculptor. Born Malaga, Spain, 1881. Lives in Paris.

158. Jacob: Saint Matorel. Galerie Simon. Paris. 1911. Etchings.

159. Jacob: Le Siège de Jérusalem. Kahnweiler. Paris. 1914. Etchings.

160. Salmon: Le Manuscrit Trouvé dans un Chapeau. Société Littéraire de France. Paris. 1919. Pen drawings.

161. Reverdy: Cravates de Chanvre. Editions Nord-Sud. Paris. 1922. Etchings.

*162. Ovid: Les Métamorphoses. Skira. Lausanne. 1931. Etchings.

*163. Balzac. Le Chef-d'oeuvre Inconnu. Vollard. Paris. 1931. Etchings and wood engravings, after drawings.

*164. Aristophanes (Seldes, translator): Lysistrata. Limited Editions Club. New York. 1934. Etchings and drawings.

ODILON REDON

Painter, graphic artist, illustrator. Born Bordeaux, France, 1840. Died Paris, 1916.

165. The Apocalypse: Vollard. Paris. n.d. Lithographs.

*166. Flaubert: La Tentation de Saint-Antoine. Vollard. Paris. In preparation. Lithographs.

167. Mallarmé: Jamais un Coup de Dé N'Abolit le Hazard. Vollard. Paris. In preparation. Lithographs.

DIEGO RIVERA

Painter. Born Guanajuato, Mexico, 1886. Lives at present in Mexico City.

168. Rivas: Cuauhtémoc. Published by the author. Mexico City. 1925. Drawings.

169. Chase: Mexico. Macmillan. New York. 1931. Drawings.

BOARDMAN ROBINSON

Painter. Born Somerset, Nova Scotia, 1876. Lives in Colorado Springs.

170. Dostoyevsky: The Brothers Karamazov. Random House. New York. 1933. Drawings.

*171. Dostoyevsky: The Idiot. Random House. New York. 1935. Drawings.

AUGUSTE RODIN

Sculptor. Born Paris, 1840. Died Paris, 1917.

172. Mirbeau: Le Jardin des Supplices. Vollard. Paris. 1902. Compositions, after drawings.

*173. Ovid: Elégies Amoureuses. Gonin. Paris. 1935. Wood engravings, after drawings.

GEORGES ROUAULT

Painter, writer. Born Paris, 1871. Lives near Paris.

*174. Rouault: Paysages Légendaires. Editions Porteret. Paris. 1929. Lithographs and drawings.

*175. Arland: Carnets de Gilbert. Nouvelle Revue Française. Paris. 1931. Colored lithographs.

176. Vollard: Réincarnation du Père Ubu. Vollard. Paris. 1933. Etchings and wood engravings, after drawings.

*177. Rouault: Le Cirque de l'Etoile Filante. Vollard. Paris. In preparation. Color etchings, and wood engravings after drawings.

178. Suarès: Cirque. Vollard. Paris. In preparation. Color etchings, and wood engravings after drawings.

179. Rouault: Guerre. Vollard. Paris. In preparation. Copper engravings.

180. Rouault: Miserere. Vollard. Paris. In preparation. Copper engravings.

181. Suarès: Passion. Vollard. Paris. In preparation. Color etchings and wood engravings.

PIERRE ROY

Painter. Born Nantes, France, 1880. Lives in Paris.

*182. Comptines. Jonquière. Paris. 1926. Stencil-colored wood engravings.

ALEKSANDR NIKOLAYEVICH SAMOKHVALOV

Painter. Born 1894. Studied, Leningrad Academy of Fine Arts. Lived in Leningrad in 1933.

*183. Saltikov-Shedrin: Istoria Odnogo Goroda (The Story of a City). Academia. Moscow. 1935. Lithographs.

ANDRE DUNOYER DE SEGONZAC

Painter, etcher. Born Boussy-Saint-Antoine (Quercy), France, 1885. Lives in Paris.

184. Dorgeles: Les Croix de Bois. Editions de la Banderole. Paris. 1921. Etchings.

185. Bernard: Le Tableau de la Boxe. Nouvelle Revue Française. Paris. 1922. Etchings.

*186. Philippe: Bubu de Montparnasse. Les Trent. Lyons. 1928. Etchings.

*187. Gignoux: L'Appel du Clown. Published by the author. Paris. 1931. Etchings.

188. Colette: La Treille Muscate. Published by the author. Paris. 1932. Etchings.

*189. Virgil: Georgiques. Vollard. Paris. In preparation. Etchings.

MAX SLEVOGT

Painter, illustrator. Born Landshut (Bavaria), 1868. Studied, Munich Academy and in Italy. One of leaders of German "Secession" and north German Impressionists. Late years devoted chiefly to graphic arts. Died near Landau, Germany, 1932.

190. Homer: Iliad. B. Cassirer. Berlin. 1906. Lithographs.

*191. Goethe, translator: Benvenuto Cellini. P. Cassirer. Berlin. 1913. Lithographs.

192. Inseln Wak Wak. B. Cassirer. Berlin. n.d. Lithographs.

193. Mozart: Zauberflöte. Marees Gesellschaft. Munich. 1920. Watercolors.

194. Grimm Brothers: Das Märchenbuch, Der Treue Johannes. B. Cassirer. Berlin. 1922. Drawings.

195. Grimm Brothers: Das Märchenbuch, König Drosselbart. B. Cassirer. Berlin. 1923. Drawings.

JOHN SLOAN
Painter, etcher. Born Lock Haven, Pennsylvania, 1871. Lives in New York.

*196. Norris, translator: The Works of Charles Paul de Kock. Quinby. New York. 1903-05. Etchings.

DAVID PETROVICH STERENBERG
Painter, etcher. Born Zhitomir, Russia, 1881. Studied in Paris, 1906. Professor, High School for Art and Industry, Moscow. Lived in Moscow, 1930.

*197. Kipling (Marshak, translator): 40 North-50 West. Molodaya-Gvardia. Moscow and Leningrad. 1931. Wood engravings.

VLADIMIR EVGRAFOVICH TATLIN
Painter, constructivist, designer for theatre. Born Moscow, 1885. Lives in Moscow.

198. Harms: Vo-Pirvikh I Vo-Vtorikh. Giz. Moscow and Leningrad. 1929. Drawings.

PAVEL TCHELITCHEW
Painter. Born Moscow, 1898. Stage settings, Berlin, 1921-23. Paris, 1923. First exhibition, Paris, 1925. Settings for Diaghileff Ballet *Ode,* 1928; for *Errante,* New York, 1933. Divides his time between New York and Paris.

199. Wescott: A Calendar of Saints for Unbelievers. Harrison of Paris. Paris. 1932. Drawings.

199A. Two original drawings for *A Calendar of Saints for Unbelievers.*

BORIS BORISOVICH TITOV
Painter. Born, 1897. Lived in Moscow in 1930.

200. Kamenski: Emel'yan Pugachev. Federatzia. Moscow. 1932. Drawings.

HENRI DE TOULOUSE-LAUTREC
Painter, graphic artist. Born Albi (Tarn), France, 1864. Died Malromé, 1901.

*201. Renard: Histoires Naturelles. Librairie Floury. Paris. 1899. Lithographs.

*202. E. de Goncourt: La Fille Elisa. Librairie de France. Paris. 1931. Facsimile with watercolors and sketches.

NIKOLAI ANDREYEVICH TYRSA
Painter. Born Aralykh (province of Erivan), Russia, 1887. Lived in Leningrad in 1934.

203. Marshak: Otryad (The Detachment). Giz. Leningrad. 1930. Color drawings.

204. Bianchi: Vesnie Domishki (Little Nests). Molodaya-Gvardia. Leningrad. 1935. Color lithographs.

VIKTOR MIKHAILOVICH VASNETZOV

Painter. Born Ryabovo (province of Vyatka), Russia, 1848. Studied, Academy of Fine Arts, St. Petersburg, 1867. Died 1926.

    205. Bianchi: Boloto (The Swamp). Molodaya-Gvardia. Leningrad. 1931. Lithographs.

MAURICE VLAMINCK

Painter. Born Paris, 1876, of Flemish parents. Lives at Rueil-la-Gadelière (Eure-et-Loire), France.

    206. Vanderpyl: Voyages. Galerie Simon. Paris. 1920. Woodcuts.

    207. Vlaminck: Communications. Galerie Simon. Paris. 1921. Woodcuts.

    207A. Duhamel: Trois Journées de la Tribu. Nouvelle Revue Française. Paris. 1921. Lithographs and woodcuts.

    208. Radiguet: Le Diable au Corps. Seheur. Paris. 1926. Lithographs.

    209. Reuillard: Grasse Normandie. Delpeuch. Paris. 1926. Drawings.

VOLSHTEIN

Painter. Russian contemporary.

    210. Leto: Kolkhoze. Giz. Leningrad. 1930. Crayon drawings.

MAX WEBER

Painter. Born Vialostok, Russia, 1881. Lives at Great Neck, New York.

    211. Weber: Primitives. Spiral Press. New York. 1926. Wood engravings.

GRANT WOOD

Painter. Born Anamosa, Iowa, 1892. Lives in Iowa City, Iowa.

    *212. Horn: The Farm on the Hill. Scribner. New York. 1936. Crayon drawings.

SOLOMON BORISOVICH YUDOVIN

Painter. Born, 1894. Studied, Vitebsk, Russia, under Pen. Lived in Leningrad in 1933.

    213. Rakovski: Bludni Bes (The Lewd Devil). Iz-Vo. Pisatelei. Leningrad. 1931. Wood engravings.

SELECTED BIBLIOGRAPHY

GENERAL

Arts et métiers graphiques. Paris, 1927 to date. Editor: Charles Peignot. Illustrated books are reviewed in each issue. No. 26, 1931, "Le livre d'art international," is especially valuable.

Basler, Adolphe & Charles Kunstler. Le dessin et la gravure moderne en France. Paris, Crès, 1930. (Peintres et sculpteurs.) "Les illustrateurs," p. 202-212.

Born, W. Moderne russische Graphik. (In: Die graphischen Künste, 1932, v. 55, p. 1-21.)

Byblis; miroir des arts du livre et de l'estampe. Paris, 1921-31. 10 v. Editor: Pierre Gusman.

Hesse, Raymond. Le livre d'art au XIXe siècle à nos jours. Paris, La Renaissance du livre, [1926]. (À travers l'art français.)

Mahé, Raymond. Bibliographie des livres de luxe de 1900 à 1928 inclus.

Paris, Kieffer, 1931 ff. V. 1, A-E, 1931; v. 2, F-M, 1933; further volumes in preparation.

Portenaar, Jan. The art of the book and its illustration. London, Harrap, [1935]. Chapter XII: "The artist as illustrator: technical processes."

Pouterman, J. E. Ambroise Vollard. (In: Arts et métiers graphiques, no. 23, 1931, p. 231-237.)

Roger-Marx, C. Book illustration by lithography and etching. (In: Atelier, 1931, v.1, p.338-345.)

Un grand éditeur, Ambroise Vollard. (In: Plaisir de bibliophile, 1930-31, v.6, p.195-210.)

La renaissance de la gravure sur cuivre dans le livre contemporain. (In: Art et décoration, 1931, v.59, p.65-74.)

Scheffler, Karl. Die impressionistische Buchillustration in Deutschland. Berlin, Berliner Bibliophilenabend, 1931.

INDIVIDUAL ILLUSTRATORS

ALTMAN, NATAN ISAYEVICH. J. E. Pouterman. Nathan Altman. (In: Arts et métiers graphiques, no.30, 1932, p.32-35.)

BACON, PEGGY. Peggy Bacon—etcher, engraver and illustrator. (In: Index of twentieth century artists, 1934, v.2, p.12-15.)

BARLACH, ERNST. Carl Dietrich Carls. Ernst Barlach; das plastische, graphische und dichterische Werk. Berlin, Rembrandt-Verlag, 1931.

BONNARD, PIERRE. J. Cassou. Bonnard. (In: Arts et métiers graphiques, no. 46, 1935, p.9-18.)

Charles Terasse. Bonnard. Paris, Floury, 1927.

BOURDELLE, ANTOINE. C. Saunier. Antoine Bourdelle décorateur de livres. (In: Amour de l'art, 1927, v.8, p.69-74.)

CHAGALL, MARC. Oeuvres illustrées par Chagall. (In: Sélection, cahier no. 6, 1929, p.60-62.)

CORINTH, LOVIS. Karl Schwarz. Das graphische Werk von Lovis Corinth. Berlin, Curlitt, 1917.

DEGAS, EDGAR. Loys Delteil. Edgar Degas. (Le peintre graveur illustré, XIXe et XXe siècles. Tome 9. Paris, 1919.)

M. Dormy. Les monotypes de Degas. (In: Arts et métiers graphiques, no. 51, 1936, p.33-38.)

DENIS, MAURICE. François Fosca. Maurice Denis et son oeuvre. Paris, Librairie Gallimard, 1924. (Les peintres français nouveaux.) "Catalogue des principales oeuvres," p.15-19.

DERAIN, ANDRÉ. G. Gabory. André Derain, lithographe, xylographe, aquafortiste. (In: Arts et métiers graphiques, no. 21, 1931, p.119-126.)

DESPIAU, CHARLES. C. Roger-Marx. Despiau, dessinateur et illustrateur. (In: Arts et métiers graphiques, no. 37, 1933, p.7-13.)

DUFY, RAOUL. F. Fleuret. Raoul Dufy, illustrateur. (In: Arts et métiers graphiques, no. 3, 1928, p.143-151.) "Livres illustrés par Raoul Dufy," p.152.

GAUGUIN, PAUL. Marcel Guérin. L'oeuvre gravé de Gauguin. Paris, Floury, 1927. 2v.

GILL, ERIC. Engravings by Eric Gill; a selection . . . with a complete chronological list of engravings. Bristol, Cleverdon, 1929.

GRIS, JUAN. Waldemar George. Juan Gris. Paris, Gallimard, 1931. (Les peintres français nouveaux, no. 44.) "Livres illustrés par Juan Gris," p. 13-14.

GROMAIRE, MARCEL. Livres illustrés par Gromaire. (In: Sélection, cahier no. 9, 1930, p.23.)

GROSZ, GEORGE. Léon Bazalgette. George Grosz, l'homme et l'oeuvre. Paris, Écrivain réunis, [192–].

HUGO, JEAN. L. Farnoux-Reynaud. Jean Hugo et l'éternelle jeunesse. (In: Arts et métiers graphiques, no. 19, 1930, p. 27-31.)

KANDINSKY, VASILY. Catalogue des oeuvres graphiques. (In: Sélection, cahier no. 14, 1933, p. 28-30.)

KAUFFER, EDWARD MCKNIGHT. Who's who, 1936. London, Black, 1936. "List of illustrations," p.1819-1820.

KENT, ROCKWELL. Rockwellkentiana; a few words and many pictures by R. K. and, by Carl Zigrosser, a bibliography and list of prints. New York, Harcourt, Brace, 1933.

KIRCHNER, ERNST LUDWIG. Gustav Schiefler. Die Graphik Ernst Ludwig Kirchners. Berlin-Charlottenberg, Euphorion Verlag, 1926-31. 2 v.

KOKOSCHKA, OSKAR. P. Westheim. Oskar Kokoschka. Berlin, Cassirer, 1925. 2d ed.

LAPRADE, PIERRE. L. G. Cann. Pierre Laprade. (In: The arts, 1929, v.15, p. 155-162, 218.) "Pierre Laprade: prints and illustrations," p.218.

C. Roger-Marx. Pierre Laprade. (In: La renaissance, 1932, v. 15, p.65-68.) "Livres illustrés de dessins," p.68.

LAURENCIN, MARIE. F. Fleuret. Marie Laurencin. (In: Arts et métiers graphiques, no. 9, 1929, p.543-548.) "Livres illustrés par Marie Laurencin," p.548.

LEBEDEFF, VLADIMIR. A. Beucler. Lebedeff. (In: Arts et métiers graphiques, no. 15, 1930, p.900-905.)

LEGRAND, EDY. D. P. Bliss. The engraved work of Edy Legrand. (In: Print collector's quarterly, 1932, v. 19, p.116-134.)

C. Vildrac. Edy Legrand. (In: Arts et métiers graphiques, no. 18, 1930, p. 1028-1032.)

LIEBERMANN, MAX. Gustav Schiefler. Max Liebermann; sein graphisches Werk. Berlin, Cassirer, 1923. 3d ed.

LYDIS, MARIETTE. H. Ankwicz von Kleehoven. Mariette Lydis. (In: Die graphischen Künste, 1932, v. 55, no. 2-3, p.65-68.)

H. de Montherlant. Mariette Lydis. (In: Arts et métiers graphiques, no. 20, 1930, p.81-87.) "Bibliographie des ouvrages illustrés par Mariette Lydis," p.87.

MAILLOL, ARISTIDE. L. G. Cann. The engraved work of Maillol. (In: The arts, 1928, v. 14, p.200-203.)

MANET, ÉDOUARD. Étienne Moreau-Nélaton. Manet graveur et lithographe. Paris, "Peintre-graveur illustré," 1906.

C. Roger-Marx. Manet illustrateur. (In: Arts et métiers graphiques, no. 30, 1932, p.18-22.)

MASEREEL, FRANS. Luc Durtain. Frans Masereel. Paris, Vorms, 1931. "Bibliographie établie par H. C. von der Gabelentz," p.61-75.

MATISSE, HENRI. C. Roger-Marx. L'oeuvre gravé d'Henri-Matisse. (In: Arts et métiers graphiques, no. 34, 1933, p. 35-38.)

MOREAU, LUC-ALBERT. C. Roger-Marx. The lithographs of Luc-Albert Moreau. (In: Print collector's quarterly, 1930, v. 17, p.260-278.) "List of works ... illustrated by Luc-Albert Moreau," p.278.

NASH, PAUL. J. G. Fletcher. The wood-engravings of Paul Nash. (In: Print collector's quarterly, 1928, v. 15, p. 209-233.) "A chronological list of wood-engravings of Paul Nash," p. 224-233.

NIVINSKI, IGNATZ. P. Ettinger. The etchings of Ign. Nivinski. (In: Studio, 1927, v. 93, p.400-403.)

PASCIN, JULES. A. Salmon. Pascin. (In: Arts et métiers graphiques, no. 20, 1930, p.64-71.)

PICASSO, PABLO. Bernhard Geiser. Picasso peintre-graveur. Berne, L'Auteur, 1933. "Livres illustrés et livres ornés de portraits d'auteurs," on pages following catalog.

REDON, ODILON. André Mellerio. Odilon Redon. Paris, Société pour l'étude de la gravure française, 1913.

RODIN, AUGUSTE. Loys Delteil. Rodin. (In his: Le peintre graveur illustré, XIXe et XXe siècles. Tome 6. Paris, 1910.)

C. Roger-Marx. Rodin dessinateur et graveur. (In: Arts et métiers graphiques, no. 25, 1931, p.349-356.) "Livres illustrés par Rodin," p.356.

ROUAULT, GEORGES. M. Dormoy. Georges Rouault. (In: Arts et métiers graphiques, no. 48, 1935, p.25-30.)

SEGONZAC, ANDRÉ DUNOYER DE. Paul Jamot. Dunoyer de Segonzac. Paris, Floury, 1929. "Albums de dessins et illustrations de livres," p.234.

C. Roger-Marx. Les dessins et les gravures de Dunoyer de Segonzac. (In: Arts et métiers graphiques, no. 6, 1928, p.361-368.) "Ouvrages illustrés par Dunoyer de Segonzac," p. 368.

SLEVOGT, MAX. Bruno Cassirer. Max Slevogt; ein Verzeichnis der von ihm illustrierten Bücher, Mappenwerke und Graphiken erscheinen im Verlag Bruno Cassirer. Berlin, Cassirer, [1924].

Emil Waldmann. Max Slevogts graphischen Kunst. Dresden, Arnold, 1921. (Arnolds graphischen Bücher, 1. Folge, Bd. 4.)

SLOAN, JOHN. A. E. Gallatin. Certain contemporaries. New York & London, Lane, 1916. "Catalogue of the etchings and lithographs of John Sloan," p.28-30.

TOULOUSE-LAUTREC, HENRI DE. Loys Delteil. H. de Toulouse-Lautrec. (Le peintre-graveur illustré, XIXe et XXe siècles. Tomes 11-12. Paris, 1920.)

Maurice Joyant. Henri de Toulouse-Lautrec. Tome 2: Dessins, estampes, affiches. Paris, Floury, 1927.

VLAMINCK, MAURICE DE. C. Roger-Marx. Vlaminck illustrateur. (In: Plaisir de bibliophile, 1927, v. 3, p.74-82.) "Ouvrages illustrés par Vlaminck," p.82.

TWO THOUSAND FIVE HUNDRED COPIES OF THIS CATALOG WERE DESIGNED AND PRINTED IN APRIL, 1936, BY WILLIAM E. RUDGE'S SONS FOR THE TRUSTEES OF THE MUSEUM OF MODERN ART.